SELECTED PLAYS
1984–87

Václav Havel was born in Czechoslovakia in 1936. Among his plays, those best known in the West are *The Garden Party*, *The Increased Difficulty of Concentration*, *The Memorandum*, *Largo Desolato*, *Temptation*, and three one-act plays: *Audience*, *Private View*, and *Protest*. He is a founding spokesman of Charter 77 and the author of many influential essays on the nature of totalitarianism and dissent, including 'An Open Letter to Dr Husák' and 'The Power of the Powerless'. In 1979 he was sentenced to four and a half years in prison for his involvement in the Czech human rights movement; out of this imprisonment came his book of letters to his wife, *Letters to Olga* (1988). In January 1983, for reasons of health, he was released from prison before his sentence was completed. In 1986 he was awarded the Erasmus Prize, the highest cultural award in the Netherlands. In November 1989 he helped to found the Civic Forum, the first legal opposition movement in Czechoslovakia in forty years; and in December 1989 he was elected President of Czechoslovakia. He is now first President of the Czech Republic.

by the same author

LIVING IN TRUTH
LETTERS TO OLGA
DISTURBING THE PEACE
OPEN LETTERS

plays
SELECTED PLAYS 1963–83
The Garden Party
The Memorandum
The Increased Difficulty of Concentration
Audience
Unveiling
Protest
Mistake

THE VANEK PLAYS

VÁCLAV HAVEL
Selected Plays
1984–87

faber and faber
LONDON · BOSTON

This collection first published in 1994
by Faber and Faber Limited
3 Queen Square London WCIN 3AU

Printed in England by Clays Ltd, St Ives plc

Published by permission of Rowholt Verlag GmbH

All rights whatsoever in these plays are strictly reserved and permission to
perform them, etc., must be made in advance, before rehearsals begin, to:
Largo Desolato: Peters, Fraser & Dunlop 503/4 The Chambers, Chelsea Harbour,
Lots Road, London SW10 OXF
Temptation and *Redevelopment*: Casarotto Ramsay Ltd, National House,
60–66 Wardour Street, London W1Z 3HP

A CIP record for this book is available
from the British Library

ISBN 0-571-17211-3

2 4 6 8 10 9 7 5 3 1

Contents

LARGO DESOLATO 1
Translated by Tom Stoppard

TEMPTATION 61
Translated by George Theiner

REDEVELOPMENT 137
Translated by James Saunders

LARGO DESOLATO

A Play in Seven Scenes

English version by
TOM STOPPARD

Author's dedication

for Tom Stoppard

The first production of this English text was at the Bristol Old Vic on 9 October 1986 when the cast was as follows:

PROFESSOR LEOPOLD NETTLES — John McEnery
SUZANA — Amanda Murray
LUCY — Meg Davies
EDWARD — Michael Bangerter
BERTRAM — Barrie Cookson
MARGUERITE — Edita Brychta
FIRST CHAP AND SECOND SIDNEY — Pavel Douglas
SECOND CHAP AND FIRST SIDNEY — Robert Hamilton

Directed by Claude Whatham

The naming of the characters, who needless to say have Czech names in the original, follows the Anglicization used in Bristol. For reasons which were initially to do with economics, the two 'Sidneys' and the two 'Chaps' were played by the same actors. This is not Havel's intention, although it was done with his permission.

CHARACTERS

PROFESSOR LEOPOLD NETTLES
EDWARD
SUZANA
FIRST SIDNEY
SECOND SIDNEY
LUCY
BERTRAM
FIRST CHAP
SECOND CHAP
FIRST MAN
SECCND MAN
MARGUERITE

The whole play takes place in Leopold's and Suzana's living room. It is a spacious room and all the other rooms in the flat lead off it. On the left there is the front door of the flat. The door has a peep-hole. In the back wall, on the left, there is a glass-panelled door leading to a balcony. In the middle of the wall there is a glass-panelled door leading to the kitchen. To the right of that there is a small staircase leading to the door of Suzana's room. On the right hand side, opposite the front door, there is a door leading to the bathroom, and a further door leading to Leopold's room. Between the doors the walls are covered with bookcases and bookshelves. There is a hat-stand near the front door. In the right hand half of the room there is a sofa with a low table in front of it, and a few chairs. On the table there is a large bottle of rum and a glass which LEOPOLD keeps filling up throughout the play and from which he keeps sipping. This is an old and solidly bourgeois apartment but the furnishings indicate that the occupant is an intellectual. Impressive orchestral music is heard at the beginning and the end of the play and also during the intervals between the scenes.

SCENE ONE

As the music dies away the curtain rises slowly.

   LEOPOLD *is alone on the stage. He is sitting on the sofa and staring at the front door. After a long pause he gets up and looks through the peep-hole. Then he puts his ear to the door and listens intently. After another long pause the curtain drops suddenly and at the same time the music returns.*

SCENE TWO

As the music dies away the curtain rises slowly.

   LEOPOLD *is alone on the stage. He is sitting on the sofa and staring at the front door. After a long pause he gets up and looks through the peep-hole. Then he puts his ear to the door and listens intently. After another long pause the curtain drops suddenly and at the same time the music returns.*

SCENE THREE

As the music dies down the curtain rises slowly.

   LEOPOLD *is alone on the stage. He is sitting on the sofa and staring at the front door. After a long pause he gets up, goes to the door and looks through the peep-hole and then he puts his ear to the door and listens intently. He evidently hears something which makes him jump back. At the same moment the door bell rings.* LEOPOLD *hesitates for a moment and then cautiously approaches the door and looks through the peep-hole. That calms him and he opens the door.* EDWARD *enters.*

LEOPOLD: At last!

EDWARD: Has anything happened?

LEOPOLD: No – *

EDWARD: Were you worried?

Translator's footnote: the use of dashes rather than full stops at the end of speeches is Havel's punctuation.

5

LEOPOLD: I feel better when there's someone here. Come in –
(EDWARD *comes forward.* LEOPOLD *closes the door behind him.*)
What's it like outside?

EDWARD: Stifling –

LEOPOLD: Lots of people?

EDWARD: No more than usual –
(EDWARD *goes to the door leading to the balcony.*)

EDWARD: Do you mind if I open it a bit?

LEOPOLD: Go ahead –
(EDWARD *opens the balcony door wide.*)
What will you have?

EDWARD: Thanks, nothing for the moment –
(LEOPOLD *sits down on the sofa.* EDWARD *takes a chair. A short pause.*)
How did you sleep?

LEOPOLD: Essentially well. I would put it at six hours net. I woke up twice but only because I needed to pee –

EDWARD: No diarrhoea?

LEOPOLD: On the contrary –

EDWARD: How about dreams?

LEOPOLD: Nothing memorable, evidently. (*Pause.*) Do you mind if I close it now?

EDWARD: Leave it open for a while. (*Pause.*) So you're all right?

LEOPOLD: At first glance I would seem to have no reason to complain today. But in all honesty I couldn't assert that I'm feeling up to the mark –

EDWARD: Nervous?

LEOPOLD: Well, I'm always nervous –

EDWARD: And the shakes you had yesterday? All gone?

LEOPOLD: I'm afraid not. In fact they're worse. It's almost as though I'd caught a chill. (*He pauses suddenly.*) Is that somebody coming?
(*They both listen quietly.*)

EDWARD: Nothing. Everything's okay –

LEOPOLD: And on top of that I've got complications – a touch of vertigo, suggestion of an upset stomach, tingling in the joints, loss of appetite, and even the possibility of constipation –

6

EDWARD: You mean you didn't go this morning?

LEOPOLD: No –

EDWARD: Are you sure it isn't just a hangover?

LEOPOLD: My condition has some similarities to a hangover but it's not a hangover, in as much as I hardly touched a drop yesterday –

EDWARD: Well, perhaps there's something wrong with you.

LEOPOLD: No, I'm afraid not –

EDWARD: Well, that's something to be grateful for isn't it?

LEOPOLD: Is it? I'd rather be ill than well like this. If only I could be sure they won't come today –

EDWARD: They can't be coming now –

LEOPOLD: Do you think so? Surely they can come any time –

(*At that moment a key rattles in the lock.* LEOPOLD *is startled.* SUZANA *comes in through the front door carrying a full shopping bag.*)

SUZANA: Hello –

(LEOPOLD *and* EDWARD *get up.*)

LEOPOLD: Hello – let me –

(LEOPOLD *takes the bag from* SUZANA *and carries it into the kitchen.*)

SUZANA: How is he?

EDWARD: The same –

(LEOPOLD *returns from the kitchen.*)

LEOPOLD: Did you get any meat?

SUZANA: Liver –

LEOPOLD: You didn't!

(SUZANA *is going up the stairs to her room.* LEOPOLD *approaches her.*)

Suzy –

(*She stops halfway up the stairs and turns towards him.*)

SUZANA: Yes?

LEOPOLD: I was up by about eight today – I felt like doing something – I was thinking of making a few notes – I had a piece of paper all ready but nothing came – I wasn't feeling up to scratch again. Those shakes I had yesterday came back – so I did a bit of tidying up, wiped out the sink, took out the rubbish, dried my towel, cleaned my comb, made myself two soft boiled eggs for lunch –

SUZANA: What did you eat them with?

LEOPOLD: Well, with a teaspoon of course –

SUZANA: A silver one?

LEOPOLD: I don't know, it might have been –

SUZANA: How many times have I told you not to use the silver teaspoons for eggs – you can't get them clean properly –

LEOPOLD: Oh yes, I'm sorry, I forgot. After lunch I tried to read a bit and then Edward here turned up . . .

SUZANA: In other words, not a lot –

(*She goes up another step or two.*)

LEOPOLD: Suzana –

(*She stops and turns towards him.*)

As you've managed to get some liver why don't we have a special supper. I'll make mustard sauce, open a bottle of decent wine – we'll ask Lucy as well, and I'm sure Edward would join us. I think it would be good for me to let my hair down, take my mind off things, reminisce a little . . .

SUZANA: I'm sorry, Leopold, but I've got tickets for the cinema –

LEOPOLD: How about after the cinema?

SUZANA: That's too late for me – you know I've got to be up early –

(SUZANA *goes into her room.* LEOPOLD *stands for a moment looking after her awkwardly, then returns slowly to his place, and sits down. Another pause*)

LEOPOLD: Edward –

EDWARD: Yes?

LEOPOLD: Will you think of me?

EDWARD: When?

LEOPOLD: Well, when I'm there –

EDWARD: You mustn't keep thinking about that all the time!

LEOPOLD: I don't keep thinking about it all the time. It just came into my head. I'm sorry –

EDWARD: Why don't you go for a walk once in a while?

LEOPOLD: Are you mad? Go out?

EDWARD: Why not?

LEOPOLD: And be a nervous wreck the whole time, not knowing what's going on back here?

EDWARD: Nothing's going on back here –

8

LEOPOLD: I know, but how am I going to know that if I'm gadding about somewhere else? What if they came just then?

EDWARD: They'd find you weren't at home. So what?

LEOPOLD: I couldn't possibly –

(*At that moment the doorbell rings.* LEOPOLD *jumps up in confusion.* EDWARD *gets up as well.* LEOPOLD *goes to the peephole and looks through it and then turns towards* EDWARD.)

LEOPOLD: (*Whispering*) What did I tell you!

EDWARD: (*Whispering*) Is it them?

(LEOPOLD *nods. They pause, at a loss. The bell rings again.*)

LEOPOLD: (*Whispering*) Should I open the door?

EDWARD: (*Whispering*) Yes, you have to –

(LEOPOLD *hesitates a moment, then breathes in, goes to the door and opens it decisively. The newcomers are* FIRST SIDNEY *and* SECOND SIDNEY.)

FIRST SIDNEY: Good afternoon, sir –

LEOPOLD: Good afternoon –

SECOND SIDNEY: Can we come in?

LEOPOLD: Do . . .

(FIRST SIDNEY *and* SECOND SIDNEY *come forward a few paces.* LEOPOLD *closes the door behind them. They all remain standing and looking at each other somewhat at a loss.*)

FIRST SIDNEY: You don't remember us?

LEOPOLD: I can't place you at the moment –

FIRST SIDNEY: We called on you once before, two years ago. You've obviously forgotten. I'm Sidney and he's also Sidney –

LEOPOLD: How do you do –

SECOND SIDNEY: We won't hold you up long –

LEOPOLD: (*Perplexed*) Well, do sit down –

(*They all sit down,* LEOPOLD *on the sofa, the others on the chairs.*)

FIRST SIDNEY: Is it all right to smoke?

LEOPOLD: Yes – certainly –

FIRST SIDNEY: Actually, I don't smoke myself; I was asking for Sidney here, he smokes like a chimney –

(SECOND SIDNEY *is going through his pockets but can't find*

9

any cigarettes. LEOPOLD *offers him one.* SECOND SIDNEY
takes one and lights it. There is an awkward pause.)
Do you need any paper?
LEOPOLD: Do you mean for writing on?
SECOND SIDNEY: If you need any we can get you some –
LEOPOLD: Really?
FIRST SIDNEY: Seeing as we work in a paper mill –
LEOPOLD: You do?
SECOND SIDNEY: So no problem –
(*Pause.* SUZANA *comes out of her room and down the stairs.*)
LEOPOLD: Suzana, these gentlemen are from the paper mill. It
seems they've been here before –
SUZANA: Good afternoon –
FIRST SIDNEY: Good afternoon –
(SUZANA *beckons to* EDWARD *who gets up and goes with her to
the kitchen. During the following scene both of them can be seen
through the glass-panelled door taking out various foodstuffs
from the shopping bag, putting them where they belong and,
during all this time, either discussing something in a lively way
or perhaps quarrelling. Pause*)
Oh, by the way, we've got a lot of interesting stuff from the
mill – minutes of meetings and so on – I'm sure you'd find
it interesting –
LEOPOLD: I'm sure I would –
SECOND SIDNEY: We'll bring it you –
(*Pause*)
FIRST SIDNEY: We know everything –
LEOPOLD: Every what thing?
FIRST SIDNEY: About you –
LEOPOLD: I see –
SECOND SIDNEY: What Sidney is trying to say is, we're your
fans. Not just us either –
LEOPOLD: Thank you –
FIRST SIDNEY: There's lots of people looking to you –
LEOPOLD: Thank you –
SECOND SIDNEY: We all believe that it will all turn out right for
you in the end –
LEOPOLD: Well, I'm not sure –

SECOND SIDNEY: The main thing is that you mustn't weaken –
we need you and we believe in you – you being the man you
are –

LEOPOLD: Thank you –
(*Pause.*)

FIRST SIDNEY: We're not holding you up, are we?

LEOPOLD: No –

FIRST SIDNEY: Are you sure? Because if we are, you only have to
say so and we'll push off –

LEOPOLD: You're not holding me up –
(*Pause.*)

FIRST SIDNEY: You know, I'm just an ordinary sort of bloke, a
nobody, but I can spot a few things and I've got my own
opinion and nobody can deny me that. And what I think is,
there's a lot that could be done – certainly more than is being
done at the moment –

LEOPOLD: This is it –

SECOND SIDNEY: Speaking for myself and Sidney here, we
reckon – and this is partly why we're here – to our way of
thinking not all the possibilities have been exhausted – I
would venture to say that the most promising possibilities are
still ahead of us. One has to take hold of the situation by the
scruff of the neck –

LEOPOLD: What possibilities in particular did you have in mind?

FIRST SIDNEY: Well, that would require some discussion, of
course –

LEOPOLD: Well, at least tell me what direction we ought to be
taking.

FIRST SIDNEY: Different directions all at the same time. Surely
no one knows that better than you! In short, it seems to us
that it's time to take the initiative – something that would
make them sit up.

LEOPOLD: I'm not sure that present circumstances differ
significantly from the circumstances that have prevailed up
to now, but even so I'm not *a priori* against an initiative –

FIRST SIDNEY: I'm glad we agree – who else but you could get
things going again?

LEOPOLD: Well as for *me* –

II

SECOND SIDNEY: We realize that things are probably not easy for you at the moment. But the respect in which you're held puts you under an obligation –

LEOPOLD: I know –

FIRST SIDNEY: You'll know what's best to do, after all you're a philosopher and I'm an ordinary bloke, a nobody. It goes without saying we're not forcing you – we haven't got the right, and furthermore you can't be expected to do it for everybody, all on your own, but, that said, what we think is, don't get me wrong, I'll let you have it straight, – that said, we are of the opinion that you could be doing more than you are in your place –

LEOPOLD: I'll think it over –

FIRST SIDNEY: We're only saying this because we're your fans – and not just us –

LEOPOLD: Thank you –

SECOND SIDNEY: A lot of people are looking to you –

LEOPOLD: Thank you –

FIRST SIDNEY: The main thing is that you mustn't weaken – we believe in you and we need you –

LEOPOLD: Thank you –

(*Pause.*)

SECOND SIDNEY: We're not holding you up, are we?

LEOPOLD: No –

SECOND SIDNEY: Are you sure? Because if we are you only have to say so and we'll push off –

LEOPOLD: You're not holding me up –

(*Pause.*)

SECOND SIDNEY: One could certainly do more – you just have to get hold of the situation by the scruff of the neck – and who else but you is there to get things going again?

LEOPOLD: Well, as for *me* –

FIRST SIDNEY: We have faith in you –

SECOND SIDNEY: And we need you –

LEOPOLD: Thank you –

FIRST SIDNEY: We're not holding you up, are we?

LEOPOLD: No –

FIRST SIDNEY: Are you really sure? Because if we are you only have to say so and we'll push off –

LEOPOLD: You are not holding me up. Excuse me –

(LEOPOLD *gets up and walks to the balcony door, shuts it and returns to his seat.*)

SECOND SIDNEY: The main thing is that you mustn't weaken –

LEOPOLD: (*Suddenly alert*) Just a moment –

FIRST SIDNEY: What's up?

LEOPOLD: I think somebody's coming –

SECOND SIDNEY: I can't hear anything –

FIRST SIDNEY: The respect in which you're held puts you under an obligation –

(*At that moment the doorbell rings. That startles* LEOPOLD *who gets up quickly, goes to the front door and looks through the peep-hole. He calms down and turns towards the* TWO SIDNEYS.)

LEOPOLD: A friend of mine –

(LEOPOLD *opens the door and* LUCY *comes in.*)

LUCY: Hello, Leo –

LEOPOLD: Come in, Lucy –

(LEOPOLD *closes the door and leads* LUCY *to the table.*)

LUCY: I see you've got company –

LEOPOLD: They're friends from the paper mill –

LUCY: Good afternoon –

FIRST SIDNEY: Good afternoon, miss –

LEOPOLD: Sit down –

(LUCY *sits down next to* LEOPOLD *on the sofa. There is a longer awkward pause.*)

Would you like some rum?

LUCY: You know I don't drink rum –

(*Pause.*)

LEOPOLD: How's life?

LUCY: Depressing –

LEOPOLD: Why's that?

LUCY: Loneliness.

(*Pause.*)

LEOPOLD: These gentlemen think it's time to take the initiative –

LUCY: They've got something there.

13

(*Awkward pause.*)

Did I come at the wrong moment? You were obviously in the middle of discussing something –

LEOPOLD: It's all right –

(*Awkward pause.*)

Have you had supper?

LUCY: No –

LEOPOLD: We're having liver. Would you like to stay?

LUCY: That would be lovely –

(*Another awkward pause.* LUCY *takes a bottle of pills out of her handbag. She puts the bottle on the table.*)

I've brought you some vitamins –

LEOPOLD: You never forget –

(*Awkward pause.*)

I'm told it's stifling today –

LUCY: Stifling and humid –

(*Awkward pause.*)

LEOPOLD: Edward opened the balcony door but I closed it again – I don't like draughts –

LUCY: Is Edward here?

LEOPOLD: Yes –

(*Awkward pause.* LEOPOLD *is becoming more and more nervous because both* FIRST *and* SECOND SIDNEY *are sitting there and not showing any signs of leaving. Several times he seems on the point of saying something but each time changes his mind. Finally he blurts out –*)

LEOPOLD: Well, look how the evening's coming on –

(LUCY *bursts out laughing.* LEOPOLD *presses her hand. Awkward pause. Both* SIDNEYS *sitting there apparently dumbfounded.*)

I've still got a few things to do –

(LUCY *bursts out laughing despite herself.*)

LUCY: What have you got to do?

(*She bursts out again and* LEOPOLD *kicks her under the table.*)

LEOPOLD: (*Stammering*) Things – make some notes – some supper –

(*He relapses into a long stifling silence. Then* SUZANA *followed by* EDWARD, *enters from the kitchen.*)

14

SUZANA: Lucy!

LUCY: Suzy!

(LUCY *gets up at once and goes towards* SUZANA *and they embrace*.)

Darling! How's life?

SUZANA: Never stops!

LUCY: We must have a chat – I've got so much to tell you.

SUZANA: Me too – but some other time, all right? – I'm in a rush.

LUCY: Hey, are you leaving?

SUZANA: I've got tickets for the cinema –

LUCY: What a shame – I was so looking forward to seeing you!

(FIRST SIDNEY *suddenly thumps his knees and stands up.* SECOND SIDNEY *gets up as well.* LEOPOLD *starts getting up*.)

FIRST SIDNEY: Well, we shall look in on you soon –

LEOPOLD: Fine –

SECOND SIDNEY: And we'll bring you that writing paper –

LEOPOLD: Fine –

FIRST SIDNEY: And also the stuff from the paper mill –

LEOPOLD: Fine –

SECOND SIDNEY: The main thing is – keep your chin up!

LEOPOLD: Thank you –

FIRST SIDNEY: When are you expecting them?

LEOPOLD: All the time –

SECOND SIDNEY: We're with you – stick with it! So long –

LEOPOLD: So long –

LUCY: So long –

(LEOPOLD *accompanies the* SIDNEYS *to the front door and opens the door for them. They go out.* LEOPOLD *closes the door behind them, and, completely spent, leans back against the door*.)

May I ask, who that was?

LEOPOLD: I don't know. They wanted something from me. I'm not sure what. I'm sure they mean well –

SUZANA: That sort of thing happens all the time round here – but I have to run. (*To* EDWARD) Let's go! (*To* LUCY) Bye for now –

LUCY: Bye, Suzy –

EDWARD: Bye –

(SUZANA *and* EDWARD *leave.* LUCY *and* LEOPOLD *are left alone.* LUCY *smiles at* LEOPOLD *for a moment, then takes hold of his hands, pulls him towards her and kisses him.*)

LUCY: Do you love me?

LEOPOLD: Mm.

LUCY: Really?

LEOPOLD: Really –

LUCY: Well why don't you say so sometimes without being asked? You've never once!

LEOPOLD: As you know, I avoid off-the-peg expressions –

LUCY: The simple truth is, you're ashamed of loving me!

LEOPOLD: Phenomenology has taught me always to beware of the propositional statement that lies outside demonstrable experience. I prefer to say less than I feel rather than to risk saying more –

LUCY: You think loving me is not a demonstrable experience?

LEOPOLD: We may mean different things by the word love. Perhaps, though the difference may be small the word denotes, for me, something on a higher plane than for you – Just a minute!

(LEOPOLD *leaves* LUCY *to approach the front door and looks through the peep-hole.*)

LUCY: What is it?

LEOPOLD: I thought I heard someone coming –

LUCY: I can't hear anything –

(LEOPOLD *comes back from the door and turns towards her.*)

LEOPOLD: Forgive me, Lucy, but does our love have to consist solely in this endless examination of itself?

LUCY: What do you expect when you're so evasive all the time –

LEOPOLD: It's just that like all women you long for security and men look for something higher –

LUCY: Just my luck to keep picking lovers with a permanent crick in their neck –

LEOPOLD: Don't be disgusting!

LUCY: What do you mean?

LEOPOLD: Please don't use the word lover! At least don't apply it to me –

16

LUCY: Why?

LEOPOLD: It's disgusting –

LUCY: Why?

LEOPOLD: It turns man into nothing but an ever-naked prick –

LUCY: (*Laughing*) Oh, who's being disgusting now –

LEOPOLD: Why don't you sit down?

(LUCY *sits down on the sofa.*)

Can I get you anything?

LUCY: Is there any wine?

LEOPOLD: I'll get some –

(LEOPOLD *goes into the kitchen and after a moment returns with a bottle of wine, a bottle opener and two glasses. He opens the bottle, pours wine into both glasses, takes one and* LUCY *takes the other.*)

Well, cheers!

LUCY: Cheers!

(*They both take a drink.* LEOPOLD *sits down on the sofa next to her. Pause.*)

So tell me –

LEOPOLD: What?

LUCY: What did you do today?

LEOPOLD: I don't know –

LUCY: Did you write?

LEOPOLD: I wanted to but it wouldn't come. I wasn't feeling well –

LUCY: Did you have your depression again?

LEOPOLD: That was another thing –

LUCY: You won't get rid of it till you start writing. Everybody's waiting for your new piece –

LEOPOLD: That's just the trouble –

LUCY: But you had it all worked out –

LEOPOLD: What do you mean?

LUCY: Well, just what you were telling me – that love is actually a dimension of being – it gives fulfilment and meaning to existence –

LEOPOLD: I couldn't have made it sound like such a cliché –

LUCY: No doubt you put it better –

LEOPOLD: It's funny but when I run out of excuses for putting

17

off writing and make up my mind to start, I stumble over
the first banality – pencil or pen? – which paper? – and then
this thing starts –

LUCY: What thing?

LEOPOLD: The cycle thing –

LUCY: What's that?

LEOPOLD: My thoughts just start going round in a loop –

LUCY: Hm –

LEOPOLD: Look, do we have to talk about me?

LUCY: You love to talk about yourself!

LEOPOLD: That's just what you think –

> (LUCY *puts her head on* LEOPOLD's *shoulder. He embraces her
> but they both continue to look straight ahead, absorbed in
> thought. Pause.*)

LUCY: Leopold –

LEOPOLD: Yes –

LUCY: I can help you break out of that –

LEOPOLD: How?

LUCY: You need love – real love – mad passionate love – not
that theoretical one, the one you write about –

LEOPOLD: I'm a bit old for that –

LUCY: You're not old, it's just that you've got an emotional
block – but I'll unblock you –

> (LUCY *embraces* LEOPOLD *and begins to kiss his face.*
> LEOPOLD *sits perplexed and remains quite passive. The curtain
> falls and the music returns.*)

SCENE FOUR

The music fades and the curtain rises slowly.

It is late in the evening. It is dark behind the balcony door.
BERTRAM *is sitting on the sofa.* LEOPOLD, *who is standing in the
background by the balcony door, wears a dressing gown with nothing
underneath it, and he is rather dishevelled and seems to be cold.*

BERTRAM: How long is it since you went out?

LEOPOLD: I don't know – ages –

BERTRAM: You don't go out at all then?

LEOPOLD: No –
    (*Pause.*)
BERTRAM: How much do you drink?
LEOPOLD: The same as everyone else –
BERTRAM: Starting in the morning?
LEOPOLD: As the case may be –
    (*Pause.*)
BERTRAM: How do you sleep?
LEOPOLD: It varies –
BERTRAM: Do you ever dream about them? Or dream that
    you're already there?
LEOPOLD: Sometimes –
    (*Pause.*)
BERTRAM: Leopold –
LEOPOLD: Yes?
BERTRAM: You don't doubt, do you, that we all like you –
LEOPOLD: I know –
LUCY: (*Off stage*) Leopold –
LEOPOLD: (*Calls out*) Just a minute –
    (*Pause.* LEOPOLD *is trembling with cold and rubbing his arms.*
    BERTRAM *looks through the medicines lying on the table.*)
BERTRAM: Vitamins?
LEOPOLD: Yes –
BERTRAM: Apart from vitamins are you on anything else?
LEOPOLD: Not really – why do you ask?
BERTRAM: There's some talk –
LEOPOLD: What sort of talk?
BERTRAM: Forget it –
    (*Pause.*)
BERTRAM: Quite a few people complain that you never answer
    letters –
LEOPOLD: I was never much of a letter writer –
BERTRAM: Well, there's no law about it . . . still, it's a pity that
    it lends support to the rumours –
LEOPOLD: What rumours?
BERTRAM: That you're no longer reliable, so –
LEOPOLD: I reply to anything important – perhaps something
    got lost in the post somewhere –

(*Pause.*)

BERTRAM: What did you think of that collection?

LEOPOLD: What collection?

BERTRAM: The stuff I lent you the other day –

LEOPOLD: Ah yes –

BERTRAM: Have you read it?

LEOPOLD: To tell you the truth –

BERTRAM: It's essential reading –

LEOPOLD: I know – That's exactly why I couldn't just glance
through it – There's a mood for everything – I can't just
read anything any time –
(*Pause.*)

BERTRAM: Leopold –

LEOPOLD: Yes?

BERTRAM: You don't doubt, do you, that we all like you?

LEOPOLD: I know –

LUCY: (*Off stage*) Leopold –

LEOPOLD: (*Calls out*) Just a minute –
(*Pause.* LEOPOLD *is trembling with cold and rubbing his
arms.*)

BERTRAM: Leopold –

LEOPOLD: Yes?

BERTRAM: It goes without saying it's your own business –

LEOPOLD: What is?

BERTRAM: You don't have to account to me –

LEOPOLD: What?

BERTRAM: I'm asking as a friend –

LEOPOLD: I know –

BERTRAM: Is it true that you're seeing Lucy?

LEOPOLD: It's not that simple –

BERTRAM: And how are things between you and Suzana?

LEOPOLD: We get along –
(*Pause.*)

BERTRAM: Leopold –

LEOPOLD: Yes?

BERTRAM: You don't doubt, do you, that we all like you?

LEOPOLD: I know –
(*Pause.*)

LUCY: (*Off stage*) Leopold –

LEOPOLD: (*Calls out*) Just a minute –
(*Pause.* LEOPOLD *is trembling with cold and is rubbing his arms.*)

BERTRAM: It's terrible of course to live with this nerve-racking uncertainty – we all understand that. None of us knows how we'd stand it ourselves. That's why so many people are concerned about you. You have to understand that –

LEOPOLD: I do understand –

BERTRAM: I'm not just speaking for myself – I'm really here on behalf of everyone –

LEOPOLD: Who's everyone?

BERTRAM: Your friends –

LEOPOLD: Are you an emissary?

BERTRAM: If you want to call it that –

LEOPOLD: And what are you concerned about, specifically?

BERTRAM: How shall I put it? I don't want to be hard on you or hurt you in any way but on the other hand I wouldn't be acting as your friend if I were to be less than frank –

LEOPOLD: And what are you concerned about, specifically?

BERTRAM: How should I put it? It's not simply a general issue, it's mostly about you personally –

LEOPOLD: And what are you concerned about, specifically?

BERTRAM: How should I put it? Simply, there's growing circumstantial evidence giving rise to certain speculations –

LEOPOLD: What circumstantial evidence? What speculations?

BERTRAM: Your friends – and I won't deny I include myself – we've all – for some time – and let's hope our fears are groundless – we've all – for some time – begun to question whether you might not crack under the strain – whether you'll be able to meet all the claims which, thanks to all you've done already – the claims which are made on you – that you'll be able to fulfil the expectations which – forgive me – are rightly expected of you – if you'll be, in short, up to your mission, which is to do justice to those great obligations, to the truth, to the world, to everyone for whom you set an example – set by your own work – forgive me – but quite simply we are beginning to be slightly afraid

21

that you might let us down and in so doing bring upon
yourself – forgive me – it would be bound to be so, given
your sensitivity – bring upon yourself endless agony –
(*Short pause.*)
You're not angry, are you, that I'm speaking so openly?
LEOPOLD: No – on the contrary –
(*Pause.*)
LUCY: (*Off stage*) Leopold –
LEOPOLD: (*Calls out*) Just a minute –
(*Pause.* LEOPOLD *is trembling with cold and is rubbing his
arms.*)
BERTRAM: It's terrible, of course, to live with this nerve-racking
uncertainty. We all understand that. None of us knows how
we'd stand it ourselves. That's why so many people are
concerned about you. You have to understand that –
LEOPOLD: I do understand –
BERTRAM: The more they count on you the harder it would be
for them if you failed to hold out in some way –
LEOPOLD: People are calling on me all the time – not long ago a
couple of lads from the paper mill showed up – typical
workers – ordinary people –
BERTRAM: That's certainly excellent, but, how should I put it?
LEOPOLD: What?
BERTRAM: How should I put it?
LEOPOLD: How should you put what?
BERTRAM: The question is whether a visit from a couple of
paper-mill workers – excellent though it is in itself – is
simply – or might become simply – forgive me – a kind of
inaction in action – a leftover from a world which is no
longer the case – whether you might not be playing the role
in a mechanical, superficial way to reassure yourself that
you are still the person to whom that role properly
belonged. What is at stake here is that a gap should not
open up between you and your role in society, so that your
role, which was a true reflection of your personality,
becomes a crutch to prop you up – circumstantial evidence
of a supposed continuity of personality – but spurious,
illusory, self-deceiving – by means of which you try to

22

assure the world and yourself that you are still the person
who you in fact no longer are – in short, that your role
which grew naturally out of your attitudes and your work
should not become a mere substitute, and that you don't
attach to that role, which has long since kept going
autonomously, on its own momentum, don't attach to it the
sole and lasting proof of your moral existence, and thus let
your entire human identity hang on a visit from a couple of
know-nothing workers from the paper mill –
(*Short pause.*)
You're not angry, are you, that I'm speaking so openly?
LEOPOLD: No – on the contrary –
(*Pause.*)
LUCY: (*Off stage*) Leopold –
LEOPOLD: (*Calls out*) Just a minute –
(*Pause.* LEOPOLD *is trembling with cold and rubbing his
arms.*)
BERTRAM: It's terrible of course to live with this nerve-racking
uncertainty. We all understand that. None of us knows how
we'd be able to stand it ourselves. That's why so many
people are concerned about you. You have to understand
that –
LEOPOLD: I do understand –
BERTRAM: You must believe me, too, that all I wish for is that
we're worrying about nothing –
LEOPOLD: I do believe you –
BERTRAM: And even if this danger, which we your friends
worry about, is infinitesimal, I have a duty – to you, to
myself, to all of us – to confess those worries to you –
LEOPOLD: I understand –
BERTRAM: By all the things you did and have been doing up to
now, you've earned our respect and our love, and in so
doing you have suffered a great deal. Obviously you are not
a superman, and the oppressive atmosphere in which you
have had to live is bound to have left its mark. But all that
said, I can't escape the awful feeling that lately something
inside you has begun to collapse – as if an axis that has held
you together has given way, as if the ground is collapsing

under your feet – as if you've gone lame inside – that you are tending more and more to act the part of yourself instead of being yourself. Your personal life, that vital plank, is – don't be angry – in a mess, you're lacking a fixed point out of which everything inside you would grow and develop – you're losing the strength and perhaps even the will to put your affairs in order – you're erratic – you're letting yourself be tossed about by chance currents, you're sinking deeper and deeper into a void and you can't get a grip on things – you're just waiting for what is going to happen and so you're no longer the self-aware subject of your life, you're turning into its passive object – you're obviously at the mercy of great demons but they do not drive you in any direction, they merely drive about inside you – your existence seems to have become a cumbersome burden to you and you have really settled for listening helplessly to the passing of the time. What happened to your perspective on things? To your humour? Your industry and persistence? The pointedness of your observations? Your irony and self-irony? Your capacity for enthusiasm, for emotional involvement, for commitment, even for sacrifice?! I fear for you, Leopold – I fear for us! We need you! You have no idea how we need you, we need you the way you used to be! So I am asking you to swear that you won't give up – Don't weaken! Keep at it! Get a grip on yourself! Pull yourself together! Straighten up! Leopold –

LEOPOLD: Yes?

BERTRAM: You don't doubt, do you, that we all like you?

LEOPOLD: I know –

BERTRAM: So I beg you – be again that brilliant Leopold Nettles whom everybody held on high!

(*From Leopold's room* LUCY *emerges quietly, dressed only in a candlewick bedspread, naked underneath it.*)

LUCY: Bertram –

(BERTRAM *is rather startled. He gets up quickly and looks at* LUCY *in astonishment.*)

BERTRAM: Oh, Lucy –

LUCY: Can't you see he's cold?

BERTRAM: He never mentioned it –

LUCY: Also, it's late –

BERTRAM: Yes – of course – forgive me – I'm sorry – I didn't realize – I'm just going –

LEOPOLD: You don't have to rush – stay the night if you like –

BERTRAM: No – thank you – and so long –

LUCY: So long – and don't be offended –

BERTRAM: That's quite all right – it was presumptuous of me – so long –

LEOPOLD: Cheerio and do come again some time!

BERTRAM: Glad to –

(BERTRAM *goes out through the front door. Short pause.*)

LEOPOLD: You didn't have to push him out like that –

LUCY: He would have been sitting here all night – And I want you for myself – We get so little time –

LEOPOLD: And it's not the best thing in the world that he saw you here –

LUCY: Why?

LEOPOLD: You know how much talk there'll be now –

LUCY: So what? Or are you ashamed of me?

LEOPOLD: It's not that –

LUCY: Then why do you treat me like a stranger in front of other people?

LEOPOLD: I don't, do I?

LUCY: Yes you do! I can't remember you ever taking my hand in company – touching me – not even a fond glance –

LEOPOLD: Hadn't we better go to bed?

LUCY: No –

LEOPOLD: Why?

LUCY: Because I want to have a serious talk with you –

LEOPOLD: About our relationship?

LUCY: Yes –

LEOPOLD: In that case at least fetch me a blanket –

(LUCY *goes to Leopold's room and returns in a moment with a blanket.* LEOPOLD *sits down comfortably on the sofa and wraps himself in the blanket. Short pause.*)

LUCY: I knew it wasn't going to be easy for me – you know I

25

had to make a few sacrifices – and what I am trying to say –
reluctantly but I have to say it – look, I respect your
idiosyncracies –

LEOPOLD: If you mean what happened – didn't happen – I
mean in there – (*He points to his room.*) then I've already
explained that I haven't been feeling up to the mark today –

LUCY: That's not what I meant – and if we're going to talk
about it then there's other reasons behind it –

LEOPOLD: Such as?

LUCY: You're simply blocked – you're censoring yourself –
you're afraid to give in to any emotion or experience –
you're controlling, observing, watching yourself every
minute – you're thinking about it, so in the end it's duty
instead of pleasure, and then, of course, it doesn't work –
but that's my problem – I wasn't going to talk about it
now –

LEOPOLD: About what, then?

LUCY: Everything I've done for us I've done freely and
willingly, I'm not complaining and I don't want anything in
return – I only want you to admit what is true –

LEOPOLD: What do you mean?

LUCY: We're seeing each other – we're lovers – we love each
other –

LEOPOLD: Have I ever denied it?

LUCY: Forgive me but you do everything you can to deny it, to
make it invisible, to avoid acknowledging it, you behave as
if it wasn't there –

LEOPOLD: I'm possibly more reserved about some things than I
should be, but – forgive me – you're partly to blame –

LUCY: Me? How?

LEOPOLD: You know – I'm really afraid of you –

LUCY: Me?

LEOPOLD: Your ceaseless effort to give a name to our
relationship, to make your status somehow official, and the
way you defend your territory while quietly but relentlessly
trying to enlarge it – the way you have to discuss it
endlessly – all that, quite naturally, makes me defensive. By
my reserve, by wariness, perhaps even by a mild cynicism,

26

I have been compensating for a subconscious fear of being manipulated, if not actually colonized – I reproach myself bitterly for my behaviour but I can't overcome it –

LUCY: But I ask so little of you! You must see that I live only for you and through you and all I want is for you to admit to yourself that you love me!

LEOPOLD: Hm –

LUCY: And I believe you do love me! I don't believe that you are incapable of love! I don't believe that my love is incapable of awakening love even in you! I'm on your side. Without love no one is a complete person! We only achieve an identity through the person next to us! – isn't that how you put it in your *Ontology of the Human Self*?! You'll see that if you lose your ridiculous inhibitions you'll come alive again – and even your work will go better than you can imagine!

LEOPOLD: I feel sorry for you, Lucy –

LUCY: Why?

LEOPOLD: You deserve someone better. I'm just worthless –

LUCY: I don't like you talking about yourself like that –

LEOPOLD: It's true, Lucy. I can't get rid of the awful feeling that lately something has begun to collapse inside me – as if some axis which was holding me together has broken, the ground collapsing under my feet, as if I'd gone lame inside – I sometimes have the feeling that I'm acting the part of myself instead of being myself. I'm lacking a fixed point out of which I can grow and develop. I'm erratic – I'm letting myself be tossed about by chance currents – I'm sinking deeper and deeper into a void and I can no longer get a grip on things. In truth I'm just waiting for this thing that's going to happen and am no longer the self-aware subject of my own life but becoming merely its passive object – I have a feeling sometimes that all I am doing is listening helplessly to the passing of the time. What happened to my perspective on things? My humour? My industry and persistence? The pointedness of my observations? My irony and self-irony? My capacity for enthusiasm, for emotional involvement, for commitment, even for sacrifice? The

27

oppressive atmosphere in which I have been forced to live for so long is bound to have left its mark! Outwardly I go on acting my role as if nothing has happened but inside I'm no longer the person you all take me for. It's hard to admit it to myself, but if *I* can all the more reason for you to! It's a touching and beautiful thing that you don't lose hope of making me into someone better than I am but – don't be angry – it's an illusion. I've fallen apart, I'm paralysed, I won't change and it would be best if they came for me and took me where I would no longer be the cause of unhappiness and disillusion –

(LUCY *gets up, upset, goes quickly to the balcony door. She opens it and goes out on to the balcony and stands looking out into the night with her back to the room. Soon it becomes clear that she is crying.* LEOPOLD *looks at her perplexed and after a while speaks to her.*)

Lucy –

(LUCY *doesn't react. Pause.*)

There, there, Lucy, what's the matter?

(LUCY *doesn't react. Pause.* LEOPOLD *gets up and approaches her slowly, still wrapped up in a blanket.*)

Are you crying, Lucy?

(*Pause.*)

Why are you crying?

(*Pause.*)

Don't cry!

(*Pause.*)

I didn't want to upset you – I didn't realize –

(*He has approached* LUCY *and touched her carefully on the shoulder.* LUCY *with a tear-stained face turns suddenly to him and cries out.*)

LUCY: Don't touch me!

(LEOPOLD *steps back surprised.* LUCY *comes back into the room, wiping her eyes, sobbing quietly.*)

LEOPOLD: What's the matter?

LUCY: Leave me alone –

LEOPOLD: There, there – what have I done now?

LUCY: You're a worse case than I thought –

28

LEOPOLD: How do you mean?

LUCY: All this talk – it's nothing but excuses! You sang a
different tune the first time you got me to stay with you!
You said our relationship would give you back some of your
lost integrity! – That it would renew your hope – that it
would put you back together emotionally! – That it would
open a door into a new life! You just say what suits you!
No, Leopold, you're no broken wreck, you're an ordinary
bullshit-artist – you've had enough of me and now you want
to get shot of me – so now you paint a picture of your ruin
to make me understand that there's nothing more I can
expect from you and – on top of that – to make me feel
sorry for you! You're ruined all right, but not in the way
you say – it's your dishonesty that shows how ruined you
are! And simpleton that I am, I believed that I could
awaken love in you, that I'd give you back your zest for life,
that I'd help you! You're beyond help! Serves me right –
one great illusion less –

LEOPOLD: You're being unfair, Lucy – I really am going
through a crisis – even Bertram says so –

LUCY: Please don't go on – there's no point. I'm going to get
dressed –

LEOPOLD: Don't be silly, Lucy! This is no way to part –
(LEOPOLD *tries to embrace her but she breaks free from him. At
that moment the doorbell rings. It startles them both and they
look at each other in confusion. Their quarrel is forgotten.*
LEOPOLD *throws his blanket on the sofa, goes quickly to the
front door and looks through the peep-hole. Then, completely
rattled, turns to* LUCY.)
(*Whispering*) It's them!

LUCY: (*Whispering*) What are we going to do?

LEOPOLD: (*Whispering*) I don't know – go in the bedroom – I'll
let them in –

LUCY: I'm staying here with you!
(*The doorbell rings again.* LEOPOLD *breathes in, smooths his
hair, goes to the door and opens it decisively. The* FIRST CHAP
and SECOND CHAP *enter.*)

FIRST CHAP: Good evening, Professor –

LEOPOLD: Good evening –

FIRST CHAP: I suppose you know who we are –

LEOPOLD: I suppose so –

SECOND CHAP: You thought we wouldn't come any more today, did you?

LEOPOLD: I realize you can come any time –

FIRST CHAP: We must apologize for the intrusion – you obviously had other plans for the evening –
(*The* TWO CHAPS *smile lecherously.*)

LEOPOLD: What plans I had is my own business –

SECOND CHAP: We possibly won't keep you long, it depends on you –

FIRST CHAP: It's a pleasure to meet you. According to our colleagues you're a sensible chap so with luck we'll soon come to an understanding –

LEOPOLD: I don't know what there is to understand. I've got my things ready, I just need time to get dressed –

SECOND CHAP: What's the hurry? It may not come to the worst –

FIRST CHAP: But we must ask the lady to kindly leave –

LUCY: I'm staying!

SECOND CHAP: No, you're leaving –
(LUCY *clings on to* LEOPOLD.)

LEOPOLD: My friend can't leave now –

FIRST CHAP: Why?

LEOPOLD: She's got nowhere to go –

SECOND CHAP: In that case we'll put her up for the night.

LEOPOLD: Oh no you won't!

FIRST CHAP: Watch!
(*The* FIRST CHAP *opens the front door and makes a gesture towards the corridor. The* FIRST MAN *and the* SECOND MAN *enter smartly. The* FIRST CHAP *points towards* LUCY. *The* FIRST *and* SECOND MAN *go to her and take her by the hands.* LUCY *struggles against them and* LEOPOLD *clasps her in his arms.*)

LUCY: You bastards!

LEOPOLD: Don't touch her!
(*The* FIRST *and* SECOND MAN *pull* LUCY *out of* LEOPOLD's

30

embrace and drag her towards the front door. LEOPOLD *tries to prevent them but they push him roughly away.*)

LUCY: (*Shouting*) Help!

    (FIRST *and* SECOND MAN *put their hands over Lucy's mouth and drag her out. The* FIRST CHAP *dismisses the men with a gesture and closes the door.*)

FIRST CHAP: Now that wasn't necessary was it?

    (LEOPOLD *remains silent.*)

SECOND CHAP: You don't have to worry about your girlfriend, nobody's going to harm her. As soon as she comes to her senses we'll take her home. You don't think we'd let her run around the streets in a candlewick bedspread –

FIRST CHAP: We're not inhuman, you can be sure of that –

    (LEOPOLD *closes the balcony door. He picks up his blanket and wraps himself into it and sits down rebelliously on the sofa. Short pause.*)

Do you mind if we sit down too?

    (LEOPOLD *shrugs.* FIRST *and* SECOND CHAPS *sit down on chairs. Pause.*)

We're sorry about that little incident, but don't give it another thought. We're better off this way. And it wouldn't be very nice for you to have your girlfriend see this –

    (*Pause.*)

SECOND CHAP: Miss Suzana isn't at home, then?

    (LEOPOLD *shrugs.*)

FIRST CHAP: We know she's at the cinema –

    (LEOPOLD *shrugs.*)

SECOND CHAP: Won't you talk to us?

    (LEOPOLD *shrugs.*)

FIRST CHAP: What are you writing at the moment, may one ask?

LEOPOLD: What does it matter –

FIRST CHAP: No harm in asking –

    (*Pause.*)

SECOND CHAP: When was the last time you went out?

LEOPOLD: I don't know –

FIRST CHAP: It was some time ago, wasn't it?

LEOPOLD: Hm –

31

(*Pause.* FIRST CHAP *looks through the medicines which are lying on the table.*)

FIRST CHAP: Vitamins?

LEOPOLD: Yes –

SECOND CHAP: Apart from vitamins are you on anything?

LEOPOLD: Not really – why?

FIRST CHAP: There's been some talk –

LEOPOLD: What sort of talk?

FIRST CHAP: Forget it –

(*Pause.*)

SECOND CHAP: How much do you drink?

LEOPOLD: The same as everyone else –

SECOND CHAP: Starting in the morning?

LEOPOLD: As the case may be –

(*Pause.*)

FIRST CHAP: Well look, Professor, we won't drag this out unnecessarily. We're here because we've been given the job of putting a proposition to you –

LEOPOLD: A proposition?

FIRST CHAP: Yes. As you know only too well, you're being threatened with something unpleasant which I personally wouldn't wish upon you and I don't suppose you are particularly looking forward to it yourself –

LEOPOLD: In a way it might be better than –

SECOND CHAP: Now, now, Professor, no blasphemy!

FIRST CHAP: As you've been told many times before, it's not our business to push these things to extremes – on the contrary we want to avoid confrontations, so that – if possible – things don't come to the worst –

SECOND CHAP: It's not in our interests –

FIRST CHAP: And in some cases, when there is no better alternative, we even look for ways to achieve our object without having to go down every twist and turn of the path –

SECOND CHAP: We always try to give people another chance –

FIRST CHAP: And that's why we're here. We've been given the job of notifying you that under certain conditions this whole matter could be dropped –

LEOPOLD: Dropped? How?

32

SECOND CHAP: The whole thing would be declared null and void.

LEOPOLD: Under what conditions?

FIRST CHAP: As you know, what's coming to you is coming to you because under the name of Professor Leopold Nettles you put together a certain paper –

SECOND CHAP: An essay, as you call it –

FIRST CHAP: You never denied it and in effect therefore, you brought the whole thing upon yourself – by this act of non-denial, you unmasked the perpetrator –
(*Brief pause.*)

SECOND CHAP: As a man of wide knowledge you must be aware that if the perpetrator isn't known one cannot proceed against him. This is known as the Principle of the Identity of the Perpetrator –

FIRST CHAP: In a word, if you would sign, here and now, a short statement saying that you are not Professor Leopold Nettles, author of the paper in question, then the whole thing will be considered null and void and all previous decisions rescinded –

LEOPOLD: If I understand you correctly you want me to declare that I am no longer me –

FIRST CHAP: That's a way of putting it which might do for a philosopher but of course from a legal point of view it doesn't make sense. Obviously it is not a matter of you declaring that you are no longer you, but only declaring that you are not the same person who is the author of that thing – essentially it's a formality –

SECOND CHAP: One name being like another name –

FIRST CHAP: Or do you think that Nettles is such a beautiful name that you couldn't bear to lose it? You only have to look in the phone book to see how many equally nice names there are –

SECOND CHAP: ⎫
FIRST CHAP: ⎭ And most of them even nicer –

LEOPOLD: Do you mean that I have to change my name?

SECOND CHAP: Not at all! You can have whatever name you like, that's entirely up to you – nobody – at least in this

33

instance – could care less. The only thing which is important here is whether you are or are not the Nettles who wrote that paper –

FIRST CHAP: If you insist on keeping your name for sentimental reasons then by all means keep it –

SECOND CHAP: Though there's no denying that it would be neater if you were to decide otherwise –

FIRST CHAP: It would be neater but it's not essential. After all there could be more than one Leopold Nettles –

SECOND CHAP: There are three just in the phone book –

FIRST CHAP: In other words, it is not so much a question of whether you are Nettles or Nichols but rather whether you are the Nettles who wrote the paper –

SECOND CHAP: You have to admit it's a good offer –

LEOPOLD: I don't understand what you'll achieve by it – or why, in that case, you're proposing it – as far as I know you never do anything without a reason –

FIRST CHAP: Our interest is to wipe this unpleasant business off the slate and give you one more chance –

LEOPOLD: What chance?

FIRST CHAP: To keep out of trouble until the next time –

LEOPOLD: I don't like it much –

FIRST CHAP: Now look, whether you like it or not is your own affair. Nobody is forcing you to do anything, and nobody can force you. But I'm telling you man to man that you'd be making a mistake if you didn't go along with it –

SECOND CHAP: It's a free gift!

FIRST CHAP: No one will know a thing so long as you don't go prattling on about it, and even if it gets around everyone will understand why you did it –

SECOND CHAP: They'd all do exactly the same –

FIRST CHAP: Many of them have already done it – and what harm has it done them? None –

SECOND CHAP: If you're hesitating then the only explanation I can think of is that you have no idea what's coming to you – (*Pause.*)

LEOPOLD: Would I have to do it right this minute?

FIRST CHAP: It would be best of course –

34

LEOPOLD: No, – this is definitely serious enough to require some reflection –

SECOND CHAP: If you want to take the risk –

LEOPOLD: What risk?

FIRST CHAP: Look, we've been given the job of notifying you of what we have notified you. We don't make the decisions –

SECOND CHAP: We're small fry –

FIRST CHAP: And we can't be expected to know, of course, what the relevant authorities will make of this whole business –

SECOND CHAP: All we can do is pass on your request for time to consider –

LEOPOLD: But surely it can't make much difference to them whether it's going to be today or the day after tomorrow!

FIRST CHAP: You must understand that their goodwill is not some kind of balloon which can be expanded indefinitely –

LEOPOLD: I do understand –

(*Longer pause.* LEOPOLD *has been rattled by all this and furthermore he's evidently becoming cold again in spite of the fact that he is wrapped up in the blanket. After a while the* SECOND CHAP *suddenly says in a loud voice.*)

SECOND CHAP: Don't be a fool, man! Here's a chance – with one stroke of the pen – to rid yourself of everything that's piled on your head, all the shit – a chance for a completely fresh start, it's once in a lifetime! What would I give for such a chance!

(*Short pause.* LEOPOLD *is openly trembling, either from nervousness or the cold.*)

LEOPOLD: (*Whispering*) Let's have a look –

(*The* SECOND CHAP *at once begins to go through all his pockets until finally in his back trouser pocket he finds a soiled piece of paper. He puts it on the table and straightens it out with the back of his hand. Then he gives it to* LEOPOLD *who holds it for a long time in his trembling hands and reads it carefully. After a while he slowly puts it back on the table and wraps himself up even more tightly in his blanket. Pause.*)

FIRST CHAP: Well, what's it to be?

(*The curtain falls, the music returns.*)

SCENE FIVE

The music fades as the curtain rises.

LEOPOLD *is alone on stage. He paces the length of the room as a prisoner might pace his cell, back and forth between the front door and the bathroom door. When he reaches the front door for the third time he pauses and looks through the peep-hole. Then he puts his ear to the door and listens intently for a moment, and then continues walking. He paces back and forth twice more and then on reaching the door he pauses, reflects a moment, then goes to one of the bookcases and from behind some books he pulls out a wooden box. He takes it to the table, sits down on a chair and opens the box. It is full of various medicines.* LEOPOLD *starts going through them, then he considers a moment, hesitates, and prepares himself a dose from several of the medicines. He tosses the dose back into his mouth, takes a drink of rum and swallows the lot. He shuts the box, puts it back behind the books and continues to pace. When he comes to the bathroom door for the second time he pauses, considers a moment, and then goes into the bathroom leaving the door open. There is the sound of running water and* LEOPOLD *gasping. Evidently he is washing his face. After a while he re-enters, his face already dry, and closes the bathroom door and continues to pace. Reaching the front door for the third time he stops and looks through the peep-hole. He then puts his ear to the door, listening intently for a while, and then continues to pace. When he reaches the front door for the second time, he pauses, considers a moment, and then goes to the bookcase where his medicines are hidden and once more takes out his box. He takes it to the table, sits down on a chair and opens the box. He starts going through his medicines, considers a moment, hesitates, prepares himself another dose of various medicines, tosses the whole lot back into his mouth, takes a drink of rum and swallows the lot. He shuts the box, puts it back behind the books and continues to pace. When he reaches the bathroom door for the second time, he pauses, considers a moment and then goes into the bathroom leaving the door open. There is the sound of running water and* LEOPOLD *gasping. He is washing his face again. After a while he re-enters, his face already dry, closes the bathroom door and continues to pace. Reaching the front door for the third time he stops, considers a moment, looks through the peep-hole, steps quickly to the place where his medicines are hidden, takes out his box, takes out one bottle of medicine, empties it into his mouth and runs into the bathroom leaving the door open. There is the sound of running water and* LEOPOLD *gasping.* LEOPOLD *re-enters after a moment, closes the bathroom door and goes quickly to the front door. He puts his ear to the door, listens for a while and suddenly leaps back. At the same moment a key rattles in the lock and through the front door comes* SUZANA *carrying a full shopping bag.*

SUZANA: Hello –

LEOPOLD: Hello –

SUZANA: Isn't Edward here?

LEOPOLD: He hasn't come yet –

> (LEOPOLD *takes the shopping bag from* SUZANA, *carries it into the kitchen and immediately returns.*)

Did you get any vegetables?

SUZANA: A cauliflower –

LEOPOLD: You didn't!

> (SUZANA *goes up the little staircase to her room.* LEOPOLD *approaches the staircase, hesitating for a moment.*)

LEOPOLD: Suzana –

> (*She stops halfway up the staircase and turns towards him.*)

SUZANA: Yes?

LEOPOLD: They were here –

SUZANA: (*Surprised*) They were?

LEOPOLD: Yes –

SUZANA: When?

LEOPOLD: During the night –

SUZANA: And how come you're here?

LEOPOLD: I'll explain –

SUZANA: Did you promise them anything?

LEOPOLD: No –

SUZANA: You didn't get into trouble again in some way, did you?

LEOPOLD: No –

SUZANA: What happened, then?

LEOPOLD: When you went out to the cinema with Edward, Lucy and I cooked ourselves that liver –

37

SUZANA: Cooked it in what?

LEOPOLD: In a frying pan –

SUZANA: Which one?

LEOPOLD: The new one –

SUZANA: And you left it in a mess –

LEOPOLD: We scrubbed it –

SUZANA: With what?

LEOPOLD: With washing powder –

SUZANA: I might have known! You know very well you shouldn't use washing powder on it –

LEOPOLD: It's all right, you can have a look – then we talked for a while and then Bertram turned up, apparently on behalf of several friends – he said they were concerned about me – that I was in a bad way – that my home life was in a mess – that I was erratic – that I wasn't doing anything –

SUZANA: I've been telling you that for ages –

LEOPOLD: When Bertram left, Lucy and I had a bit of a row –

SUZANA: What about?

LEOPOLD: It's complicated – basically she complains that I don't love her enough – that I'm evasive – that I don't make it clear in company that we belong to each other, and so on – and when I honestly tried to explain things to her she said I was making excuses –

SUZANA: Well, does that surprise you?

LEOPOLD: I know what she means but what am I supposed to do?

SUZANA: Well, if you don't know –

LEOPOLD: Before she could leave they came and then because she insisted on staying they called some men in and they dragged her away –

SUZANA: Is she out yet?

LEOPOLD: I don't know – perhaps –

SUZANA: What do you mean, you don't know? Haven't you gone to see her?

LEOPOLD: I can't possibly leave here! Not now!

SUZANA: Of course. And what about them?

LEOPOLD: Apparently I won't have to go there if I make a statement that I am not the author of that – if I say simply that I am somebody else –

SUZANA: Somebody else! That would just suit them! Denounce yourself and spit on your own work!

LEOPOLD: They are not asking me to make a value judgement, they only want a formal excuse to drop the whole thing –

SUZANA: Tsss!

LEOPOLD: They're obviously worried that once I get there it would only increase the respect in which I'm held –

SUZANA: Whereas if you were to recant you'd lose it all! Obviously that would be much more to their liking! I hope you threw them out –

LEOPOLD: I've asked for time to consider –

SUZANA: What?

LEOPOLD: There's nothing to it, surely –

SUZANA: Have you gone mad? What is there to consider? That's just showing them that they're half way to breaking you – and now they'll increase the pressure! I knew as soon as I saw you that you'd got yourself into trouble! You wet!

LEOPOLD: It's all very well for you to talk –

SUZANA: If you can't take it you should never have got into it.

(SUZANA *turns abruptly and goes towards her room.*)

LEOPOLD: Suzana –

SUZANA: (*Without looking at him*) Leave me alone –

(SUZANA *goes into her room.* LEOPOLD *nervously begins to pace his usual path. When he reaches the front door for the third time, he stops, goes to the spot where his medicines are hidden, quickly extracts his box, takes a pill out of a bottle, throws it into his mouth and swallows it. He puts the box back, then continues pacing and when he gets to the bathroom door he pauses, goes quickly to the front door, looks through the peep-hole and then runs into the bathroom leaving the door open. There is the sound of running water and* LEOPOLD'*s gasping. Suddenly the doorbell rings. Water is still running,* LEOPOLD *is gasping and obviously does not hear the bell. After a while the bell rings again. The sound of running water stops, and after a moment* LEOPOLD *comes out of the bathroom, drying his wet hair with a towel. Drying his hair he continues to pace. When he reaches the front door for the third time he looks through the*

peep-hole. At that moment the bell rings again. LEOPOLD
jumps, then he returns to the door and looks through the peep-hole. He calms down and looks through the door. EDWARD
enters wearing a dinner jacket.)

EDWARD: At last!

LEOPOLD: Has something happened?

EDWARD: I rang three times –

LEOPOLD: I was getting myself together –

EDWARD: (*Going to the balcony door*) Can I open it a bit?

LEOPOLD: Go ahead.

(EDWARD *opens the balcony door wide.* LEOPOLD, *the towel round his neck, walks slowly round the room.* EDWARD *sits down on a chair.*)

EDWARD: I'm relieved to find you here –

LEOPOLD: You know, then?

EDWARD: Lucy came to see me –

LEOPOLD: So she's out –

EDWARD: What did they want?

LEOPOLD: To negotiate –

EDWARD: Did you sign anything?

LEOPOLD: I've asked for time to consider –

EDWARD: When will they be back?

LEOPOLD: They never say –

EDWARD: You ought to go and see Lucy, she's having a bad
time one way and another –

LEOPOLD: I can't possibly leave here! Not now!

EDWARD: Is Suzana at home?

LEOPOLD: Yes – she was just asking for you –

(LEOPOLD *goes into the bathroom and after a while returns
without the towel and with his hair combed.*)

Do you mind if I close it now?

EDWARD: Leave it a while –

(LEOPOLD *returns to his place and sits down. Pause.*)

LEOPOLD: That's a nice outfit you've got on –

EDWARD: It's a dinner jacket – my uncle lent it to me –

LEOPOLD: I know it's a dinner jacket – it's nice –

EDWARD: You know my uncle – (*Pause.*) How did you sleep?

LEOPOLD: Hardly at all –

EDWARD: You couldn't get them out of your mind, could you?
LEOPOLD: Well –
   (*Pause.*)
EDWARD: Did you go this morning?
LEOPOLD: Yes –
EDWARD: Well, that's something anyway –
LEOPOLD: Not much of a thing, as it happens –
   (*Pause.*)
EDWARD: What did you eat?
LEOPOLD: I wasn't hungry, I just ate a couple of onions and five
   almonds to calm myself down –
EDWARD: And did it?
LEOPOLD: Not really –
   (*Pause.*)
EDWARD: The main thing is that you're here –
LEOPOLD: I'd rather be there than here like this! Why can't I
   get my life clear! It was wonderful when nobody was
   interested in me – when nobody expected anything from
   me, nobody urging me to do anything – I just browsed
   around the second-hand bookshops – studying the modern
   philosophers at my leisure – spending the nights making
   notes from their works – taking walks in the parks and
   meditating – why can't I change my name to Nichols, say,
   and forget everything and start a completely new life?
EDWARD: Perhaps you need some of your pills –
LEOPOLD: I splash water on my face – I don't want pills – I
   don't want to get dependent on them –
   (*Pause.* LEOPOLD *becomes alert, and listening.*)
EDWARD: Nothing –
   (*At that moment the doorbell rings.* LEOPOLD *jumps up in
   confusion.* EDWARD *also gets up.* LEOPOLD *goes to the peep-
   hole and looks through it and leaps back from the door and runs
   across the room into the bathroom leaving the door open.
   Immediately there is the sound of running water.* EDWARD *is
   puzzled. He steps to the bathroom door. Short pause.*)
   (*Whispering towards the bathroom*) Leopold, come on –
   (*Short pause and the sound of water.*)
   (*Whispering towards the bathroom*) Don't be silly, Leopold,

face up to it!

(*Short pause and the sound of water.*)

(*Whispering towards the bathroom*) I'll tell them you're not at home if you like but it would be better to get it over with –

(*Short pause and the sound of water. The bell rings again.* EDWARD *doesn't know what to do. Then he makes up his mind abruptly and goes decisively to the main door, to the front door, opens it wide and gazes with surprise.* FIRST SIDNEY *and* SECOND SIDNEY *enter each carrying a large suitcase. They put their suitcases down.*)

FIRST SIDNEY: Good afternoon –

EDWARD: Good afternoon –

FIRST SIDNEY: Isn't the professor in?

(EDWARD *is puzzled. Finally he nods, slowly closes the door and goes into the bathroom leaving the door half open. There is a short pause. The sound of water stops suddenly and there is some incomprehensible whispering for quite a long time off stage.* FIRST SIDNEY *and* SECOND SIDNEY *stand motionless next to their suitcases. Finally* LEOPOLD *comes out of the bathroom with his hair wet but sleekly combed.* EDWARD *follows him, closing the bathroom door.*)

LEOPOLD: Good afternoon –

SECOND SIDNEY: Here we are, professor –

LEOPOLD: Excellent –

FIRST SIDNEY: We've got it –

LEOPOLD: What?

(FIRST SIDNEY *and* SECOND SIDNEY *put their suitcases on the table and open them. Both suitcases are full of various documents.*)

FIRST SIDNEY: (*Pointing to his suitcase*) These are blank papers – these are normal office issue – these are for carbon copies – these are carbon papers – and here we have various envelopes and files and so on –

LEOPOLD: Is that all for me?

FIRST SIDNEY: Of course --

LEOPOLD: How much do I owe you?

FIRST SIDNEY: Do me a favour, professor, what do you take us for!

LEOPOLD: Well, thank you very much – I think that should last me –

SECOND SIDNEY: We're looking forward to what you'll be writing on these bits of paper –

FIRST SIDNEY: (*Pointing to the other suitcase*) Well, and this is the stuff from our plant – these are minutes of the board of management – these are minutes of meetings of all the paper-mill employees – these are specimens of factory correspondence – here we have various memos, internal regulations, information for the work-force, overtime summaries – and this is specially interesting, that's from the personnel department – personal records of employees – various complaints – returns – denunciations –

SECOND SIDNEY: I think it'll make very nice reading for you –

FIRST SIDNEY: Use it as you see fit –

SECOND SIDNEY: If you can do anything with it, it will certainly be a bombshell –

FIRST SIDNEY: Absolutely –

LEOPOLD: Thank you so –

(FIRST SIDNEY *takes a sheaf of papers out of one of the suitcases and looks around.*)

FIRST SIDNEY: Where do you want it?

LEOPOLD: (*Looking around*) Where? Well, in this corner, here –

(LEOPOLD *points to the left-hand corner of the room, downstage.* FIRST SIDNEY *and* SECOND SIDNEY *start taking papers from the two suitcases and carrying them to the corner where they place them on the floor. After a while they are joined first by* LEOPOLD *and then by* EDWARD. *When the contents of both suitcases are in the corner,* SECOND SIDNEY *closes both of the now empty cases and carries them to the front door. Then* FIRST *and* SECOND SIDNEY *sit down at the table.* LEOPOLD *sits down on the sofa.* EDWARD *remains standing in the background. There is a long awkward pause.*)

LEOPOLD: There's a lot of it –

SECOND SIDNEY: For you we'd steal the whole paper mill if we had to –

LEOPOLD: Thank you –

(*Awkward pause.*)

I wasn't expecting you so soon –

FIRST SIDNEY: One must strike while the iron is hot, that's
what me and Sidney always say –

LEOPOLD: Very well put –

(*Awkward pause.*)

I don't know how I'm ever going to repay you –

SECOND SIDNEY: What is there to repay? We've already told
you that we're your fans – and not just us –

FIRST SIDNEY: There's lots of people looking to you –

LEOPOLD: Thank you –

(*Awkward pause.*)

I wasn't expecting you so soon –

SECOND SIDNEY: One must strike while the iron is hot, that's
what me and Sidney always say –

LEOPOLD: Very well put –

(*Awkward pause.*)

I don't know how I'm ever going to repay you –

FIRST SIDNEY: What is there to repay? We've already told you
that we're your fans – and not just us –

SECOND SIDNEY: There's lots of people looking to you –

(*Awkward pause.*)

LEOPOLD: I don't know how I'll ever repay you –

SECOND SIDNEY: What is there to repay? We've already told
you that we're your fans – and not just us –

LEOPOLD: Excuse me –

(LEOPOLD *gets up and goes to the balcony door and closes it
and then returns to his seat.* SECOND SIDNEY *is feeling his
pockets.* LEOPOLD *offers him a cigarette.*)

SECOND SIDNEY: I've got some today –

(SECOND SIDNEY *finds his cigarettes at last and he lights one.*)

But could I ask you for something else –

LEOPOLD: I'm at your disposal –

SECOND SIDNEY: Would there be any chance of a glass of rum?

LEOPOLD: Yes – of course –

SECOND SIDNEY: Just to clarify – I'm a teetotaller – but I was
asking for Sidney here – he drinks like a fish –

(LEOPOLD *gets up and goes to the kitchen and comes back at
once with a glass. He pours rum from his bottle into the glass*

44

and hands it to FIRST SIDNEY.)

FIRST SIDNEY: Thanks! Cheers!

(FIRST SIDNEY *drinks the whole glass in one go and then burps, satisfied.* LEOPOLD *refills his glass.*)

FIRST SIDNEY: Thanks! Cheers!

(FIRST SIDNEY *drinks the whole glass in one go and then burps, satisfied.* LEOPOLD *fills his glass again.*)

Thanks! Cheers!

(FIRST SIDNEY *drinks the whole glass in one go and then burps, satisfied.* SUZANA *comes out of her room in a long evening dress and walks down the little staircase.*)

LEOPOLD: Look, Suzana, these gentlemen have brought me all this paper and all sorts of interesting stuff –

SUZANA: Where's it going to go?

LEOPOLD: I'll find somewhere – that's a nice dress.

(SUZANA *makes a sign to* EDWARD *who accompanies her to the kitchen. During the rest of the scene both of them can be seen through the glass-panelled kitchen door taking out various foodstuffs from the shopping bag, putting them where they belong, and, during all this time either discussing something in a lively way or perhaps quarrelling.* LEOPOLD *notices that* FIRST SIDNEY'S *glass is empty and fills it up again for him.*)

FIRST SIDNEY: Thanks! Cheers!

(FIRST SIDNEY *drinks the whole glass in one go and then burps, satisfied.* LEOPOLD *refills the glass.*)

Thanks! Cheers!

(FIRST SIDNEY *drinks the whole glass in one go and then burps, satisfied.* LEOPOLD *refills the glass.*)

Thanks! Cheers!

(FIRST SIDNEY *drinks the whole glass in one go and then burps, satisfied.* LEOPOLD *refills the glass.*)

Thanks! Cheers!

(FIRST SIDNEY *drinks the whole glass in one go and then burps, satisfied.* LEOPOLD *refills the glass.* FIRST SIDNEY *takes the glass but when he is on the point of drinking it he puts it back on the table.*)

FIRST SIDNEY: Someone has to be sensible –

(*Short pause.*)

SECOND SIDNEY: We're not holding you up are we?

LEOPOLD: No –

FIRST SIDNEY: Are you sure? Because if we are you only have to say so and we'll push off –

LEOPOLD: You're not holding me up – excuse me –

(LEOPOLD *gets up, goes to the place where his medicines are hidden, turns his back to the room so as not to be seen, pulls out his box, quickly takes out a pill, throws it into his mouth and swallows it and puts his box back and returns to his seat. Pause.*)

SECOND SIDNEY: Have you thought about it yet?

LEOPOLD: About what?

FIRST SIDNEY: What we were talking about yesterday – that it's time for an initiative –

LEOPOLD: Oh yes – I haven't got round to it yet –

SECOND SIDNEY: Pity. You know, I'm an ordinary bloke, a nobody, but I can spot a few things and I've got my own opinion and nobody can deny me that. And what I think is, there's a lot that could be done – certainly more than is being done at the moment –

FIRST SIDNEY: One just has to get hold of the situation by the –

SECOND SIDNEY: Who else but you is there to get things going again?

(LEOPOLD *is starting to get nervous. He looks discreetly at his watch.*)

FIRST SIDNEY: We're not holding you up are we?

LEOPOLD: No –

SECOND SIDNEY: Are you sure? Because if we are you only have to say so and we'll push off –

LEOPOLD: You're not holding me up. Excuse me –

(LEOPOLD *gets up and goes into the bathroom, leaving the door open. There is the sound of running water and* LEOPOLD *gasping. The sound of water stops and shortly afterwards* LEOPOLD *returns to his seat.*)

FIRST SIDNEY: That thing you wrote – even if we don't fully understand it –

SECOND SIDNEY: We're ordinary people –

FIRST SIDNEY: – and the fact that you're right behind it –

SECOND SIDNEY: – regardless of the consequences –

FIRST SIDNEY: – straight away leads one to hope that you will take the final step –

LEOPOLD: What final step?

SECOND SIDNEY: I'm not really good at explaining myself but let me put it like this – that whatever you're writing, you'll turn it into something that will have a practical effect –

FIRST SIDNEY: To put it simply, that you'll come up with the pay-off to all your philosophizing –

LEOPOLD: The trouble is that opinions differ about quite what the pay-off is –

SECOND SIDNEY: You'll find it –

FIRST SIDNEY: Who else but you is there to get things going again –

SECOND SIDNEY: I'd say that's just what people are waiting for –

LEOPOLD: What people?

FIRST SIDNEY: Everybody –

LEOPOLD: Isn't that a bit of an exaggeration?

SECOND SIDNEY: Forgive me but you probably don't realize –

LEOPOLD: What?

FIRST SIDNEY: Your responsibility –

LEOPOLD: For what?

SECOND SIDNEY: For everything –

(LEOPOLD *is evidently nervous. He looks at his watch.*)

FIRST SIDNEY: We're not holding you up?

LEOPOLD: No –

FIRST SIDNEY: ⎱Are you sure? Because if we are you only
SECOND SIDNEY: ⎰have to say so and we'll push off –

LEOPOLD: You're not holding me up. Excuse me –

(LEOPOLD *gets up and goes to the kitchen and returns shortly with a small plate on which there are two onions and five almonds. He eats the lot during the following dialogue.*)

SECOND SIDNEY: Sidney and I were giving it a bit of thought the other day –

FIRST SIDNEY: And we got the following idea –

LEOPOLD: What idea?

SECOND SIDNEY: We think it's quite good –

LEOPOLD: What idea?

FIRST SIDNEY: This could be exactly the step that everyone is waiting for you to take –

LEOPOLD: What?

SECOND SIDNEY: That you should write a kind of declaration –

LEOPOLD: What kind of declaration?

FIRST SIDNEY: Quite simply a kind of general declaration covering all the basics –

SECOND SIDNEY: It would have to be brief and easy to understand of course –

FIRST SIDNEY: In other words you'd have to spend some time on it –

SECOND SIDNEY: You've got plenty of paper now –

(LEOPOLD, *irritated, gets up, ambles round the room and then turns to the* TWO SIDNEYS.)

LEOPOLD: Forgive me, gentlemen, but I'm not clear about –

(SUZANA, *followed by* EDWARD, *comes out of the kitchen.* LEOPOLD *looks at them in surprise.*)

(*To* SUZANA) Are you leaving?

SUZANA: Why?

LEOPOLD: I thought that we might – since you got that cauliflower – since I need to calm down a bit – to examine everything calmly – to discuss –

SUZANA: Forgive me, Leopold, but I've got tickets for a dance – I bought them ages ago –

LEOPOLD: I see – I see –

SUZANA: It's my first dance this year –

LEOPOLD: I understand – I understand –

SUZANA: Not that I know what there is to discuss – I've already given you my opinion –

LEOPOLD: I know – I only thought – but it doesn't really matter –

SUZANA: Well, so long –

EDWARD: So long, Leopold – and get to bed soon – get some sleep –

(SUZANA *and* EDWARD *leave through the front door.* LEOPOLD *looks at them awkwardly as they leave. Pause.*)

FIRST SIDNEY: What aren't you clear about?

LEOPOLD: (*Turning round*) I beg your pardon?

SECOND SIDNEY: You were saying that you weren't clear about something –

48

LEOPOLD: Was I? Ah – yes – don't be angry, gentlemen, but I'm not really quite clear about –

FIRST SIDNEY: About what?

LEOPOLD: About what exactly you want from me –

(FIRST SIDNEY *drinks the glass of rum in one go and then gets up.* SECOND SIDNEY *gets up also. They both step nearer to* LEOPOLD.)

FIRST SIDNEY: Professor, you've obviously got us wrong – we don't want anything from you –

SECOND SIDNEY: We've only taken the liberty of giving you our opinion –

FIRST SIDNEY: It's the opinion of ordinary people –

SECOND SIDNEY: Of lots of ordinary people –

FIRST SIDNEY: We only wanted to offer a suggestion –

SECOND SIDNEY: We meant well –

FIRST SIDNEY: We can't help not being able to express ourselves exactly –

SECOND SIDNEY: We're not philosophers –

FIRST SIDNEY: We just thought you might be interested in our opinion –

SECOND SIDNEY: As representing the opinion of ordinary –

LEOPOLD: I'm not saying that I'm not interested in your opinion –

FIRST SIDNEY: Well, you seem to be implying that we're confusing you –

LEOPOLD: Really I'm not suggesting anything of the sort –

SECOND SIDNEY: You were saying that you weren't clear about what we want from you –

LEOPOLD: I don't exactly know what I was saying –

FIRST SIDNEY: But we know –

(*At that moment the bathroom door opens.* BERTRAM *is standing in the doorway talking to* LEOPOLD.)

BERTRAM: I don't want to be hard on you or hurt you in any way.

(*At that moment the kitchen door opens.* EDWARD *is standing there speaking to* LEOPOLD.)

EDWARD: Were you worried?

(*At that moment the door of Suzana's room opens.* SUZANA *is standing there speaking to* LEOPOLD.)

SUZANA: Are you sure you didn't get yourself into trouble again somehow?

BERTRAM: I'm not just speaking for myself.

EDWARD: Perhaps you should take some pills –

(*At that moment the balcony door opens.* LUCY *is standing there in her bedspread and speaking to* LEOPOLD.)

LUCY: You sang a different tune the first time you got me to stay here with you.

EDWARD: You ought to go and see Lucy.

FIRST SIDNEY: This could be what people are waiting for –

SECOND SIDNEY: You'll find a way –

SUZANA: What is there to consider, for goodness sake.

BERTRAM: And how are things between you and Suzana?

LUCY: You've had enough of me and now you want to get shot of me –

EDWARD: Did you sign anything?

FIRST SIDNEY: We've only taken the liberty of giving you our opinion –

SECOND SIDNEY: The opinion of ordinary people –

FIRST SIDNEY: Lots of ordinary people –

EDWARD: Some hero.

SUZANA: Some hero.

BERTRAM: Some hero.

LUCY: Some hero.

FIRST SIDNEY: You've had enough of me and now you want to get shot of me.

SECOND SIDNEY: Some hero.

FIRST SIDNEY: Did you sign anything?

LEOPOLD: (*Shouting*) GET OUT!

(*For a moment there is complete silence and then the doorbell rings.* LEOPOLD *runs into the bathroom.* BERTRAM *makes way for him and* LEOPOLD *disappears into the bathroom and immediately there is the sound of running water. All the people on stage disappear behind the doors through which they came.* FIRST *and* SECOND SIDNEY *disappear with their suitcases through the front door. They all go and all the doors except the bathroom door are closed. The only sound is running water and*

LEOPOLD *gasping. The doorbell rings again.*
The curtain falls as the music begins to be heard.)

SCENE SIX

The music fades as the curtain rises.

    There is no one on the stage. The bathroom door is open. There is
the sound of running water and of LEOPOLD *gasping. There is a*
short pause. Then the bell rings. The sound of water stops and
LEOPOLD *runs out of the bathroom. He was obviously having a*
shower. He is wet and is covered only by a towel wrapped round his
waist. He runs to the main door, looks through the peep-hole, is
taken aback, hesitates a moment and then opens the door.
MARGUERITE *enters.*

MARGUERITE: Good evening –
LEOPOLD: (*A bit nonplussed*) Good evening –
    (*Short pause.*)
MARGUERITE: Professor Nettles?
LEOPOLD: Yes –
    (*Short pause.*)
MARGUERITE: Sorry to disturb you –
LEOPOLD: You're not disturbing me –
MARGUERITE: I won't hold you up for long –
LEOPOLD: I've got time –
    (*Short pause.*)
MARGUERITE: My name's Marguerite. I'm a student of
    philosophy –
LEOPOLD: At the university or a private student?
MARGUERITE: Both –
    (MARGUERITE *walks to the middle of the room and looks*
    round uncertainly. LEOPOLD *closes the door. A short pause.*)
    Sit down –
MARGUERITE: Thank you –
    (MARGUERITE *sits down shyly on the edge of the sofa.*)
LEOPOLD: Would you like some rum?
MARGUERITE: No – thank you – I'm not used to rum –
LEOPOLD: One glass won't do you any harm –

(LEOPOLD *pours some rum into the glass which has remained on the table*.)

MARGUERITE: Well, thank you –

(MARGUERITE *takes a very small sip and winces*.)

LEOPOLD: Not bad is it?

MARGUERITE: No –

(*Awkward pause*.)

You'll catch cold.

LEOPOLD: Ah yes, of course –

(LEOPOLD *goes quickly into the bathroom and comes back in a moment wearing a dressing gown under which he is naked. He sits down on the sofa next to* MARGUERITE *and smiles at her.* MARGUERITE *smiles back. There is a longer awkward pause*.)

MARGUERITE: I know your work –

LEOPOLD: Really? Which?

MARGUERITE: *Phenomenology of Responsibility*, *Love and Nothingness*, *Ontology of the Human Self* –

LEOPOLD: You've read all those?

MARGUERITE: Several times –

LEOPOLD: Well, I am impressed –

(*Pause*.)

MARGUERITE: I hear *Ontology of the Human Self* got you into trouble –

LEOPOLD: It's because of that I'm supposed to go there –

MARGUERITE: What – straight there? How come?

LEOPOLD: Paragraph 511 – intellectual hooliganism –

MARGUERITE: That's awful!

LEOPOLD: That's the sort of world we're living in –

MARGUERITE: For such beautiful thoughts!

LEOPOLD: Apparently someone didn't think they were so beautiful –

MARGUERITE: And is it definite?

LEOPOLD: I could get out of it by denying that I wrote it –

MARGUERITE: Is that what they're offering you?

LEOPOLD: Yes –

MARGUERITE: They're disgusting!

(*Pause.* MARGUERITE *takes a sip and winces.* LEOPOLD *promptly fills up her glass*.)

Your essays have given me a great deal of –

LEOPOLD: Yes? I'm so glad –

MARGUERITE: It's because of them that I became interested in philosophy –

LEOPOLD: Really?

MARGUERITE: Somehow they opened my eyes –

LEOPOLD: You're exaggerating –

MARGUERITE: Really –

LEOPOLD: Have another drink –

(MARGUERITE *has a drink and winces.* LEOPOLD *promptly refills her glass. Awkward pause.*)

MARGUERITE: Are you writing anything?

LEOPOLD: I'm trying to –

MARGUERITE: Could you tell me – excuse my curiosity – could you tell me what you're writing?

LEOPOLD: I'm trying to think about love as a dimension of being –

MARGUERITE: You touched on that a little in the second chapter of *Love and Nothingness* –

LEOPOLD: That's right –

(*Awkward pause.*)

MARGUERITE: Professor –

LEOPOLD: Yes, Marguerite?

MARGUERITE: I wouldn't dare to trouble you –

LEOPOLD: You're not troubling me at all! On the contrary – I'm very pleased to have met you –

MARGUERITE: If it wasn't for the fact that I'm sure you're the only one who can help me –

LEOPOLD: What's the matter?

MARGUERITE: It's going to sound silly –

LEOPOLD: You can tell me!

MARGUERITE: I'm suddenly embarrassed –

LEOPOLD: But why, there's no need –

(MARGUERITE *has a drink and winces.* LEOPOLD *promptly refills her glass. Short pause.*)

MARGUERITE: Where should I begin? I just don't know what to do –

LEOPOLD: In your studies?

53

MARGUERITE: In my life –

LEOPOLD: In your life?

MARGUERITE: I find everything so stifling – all those hopeless
faces in the bus queues – the endless hue and cry in the
streets – people twisted out of shape in their offices and
everywhere else – the general misery of life – forgive me, I
know it's silly, you don't even know me – but I didn't know
anyone else I could turn to –

LEOPOLD: I'm delighted that you should confide in me –

MARGUERITE: I don't get on with my parents – they're middle
class types who are always watching TV – I've no boyfriend
– the other students seem terribly superficial –

LEOPOLD: I know what you mean –

MARGUERITE: You're not angry?

LEOPOLD: Why do you make excuses for yourself all the time?
What greater satisfaction could there be for a philosopher
than to receive a visit from a reader in mid-crisis about the
meaning of life?

MARGUERITE: I know that you can't solve my problem for me –

LEOPOLD: You're right in the sense that the meaning of life is
not something which one can summarize or verbalize one
way or the other and then hand over like a piece of
information – it's not an object, it's more like an elusive
spiritual state – and the more one needs it the more elusive
it becomes –

MARGUERITE: Yes, yes, that's exactly –

LEOPOLD: On the other hand there is the fact – as I've already
tried to show in *Ontology of the Human Self* – that there's a
certain non-verbal, existential space in which – and only in
which – one can get hold of something through
experiencing the presence of another person –

MARGUERITE: Forgive me, it's exactly that part – it's from
chapter four – which made me decide to come and see you –

LEOPOLD: There you are! But I wouldn't like to raise your
hopes unduly, because the fact that I'm meditating on this
subject doesn't automatically mean that I am myself capable
of creating such a space –

MARGUERITE: But you've been creating it for ages – by talking

54

to me at all – by understanding me – forgive me, I'm
probably already a bit tipsy –

LEOPOLD: Not at all! Drink up –

(MARGUERITE *takes a drink and winces.* LEOPOLD *promptly
fills up her glass.*)

LEOPOLD: I'll tell you something, Marguerite – honesty deserves
honesty: if I am able to understand you then it is mainly
because I'm in a similar or perhaps even worse situation than
you –

MARGUERITE: You? I can't believe it! You know so much –
you've achieved so much – you're so wise –

LEOPOLD: That guarantees nothing –

MARGUERITE: I'm only a silly girl, but you –

LEOPOLD: You're not silly –

MARGUERITE: I am, I know it –

LEOPOLD: You're clever, Marguerite – and not only that, you're
beautiful –

MARGUERITE: Me? Well, whatever next –

LEOPOLD: I'll be quite frank with you, Marguerite: I'm in a very
bad way –

MARGUERITE: I know life has been hard on you but you seem so
strong –

LEOPOLD: Alas, that's only appearance. In reality I've had the
feeling for some time now that something is collapsing inside
me – as if an axis holding me together has started to break –
the ground crumbling under my feet – I lack a fixed point
from which everything inside me could grow and develop – I
get the feeling sometimes that I'm not really doing anything
except listening helplessly to the time going by. Gone is the
perspective I once had – my humour – my industry and
persistence – the pointedness of my observations –

MARGUERITE: How beautifully you put it –

LEOPOLD: You should have known me before! It's all gone, my
irony, my self-irony, my capacity for enthusiasm, for
emotional involvement, for commitment, even for sacrifice!
This might disappoint you, Marguerite, but for a long time I
haven't been the person that you obviously take me for!
Basically I'm a tired, dried out, broken man –

55

MARGUERITE: You mustn't speak like that, Professor! You're too hard on yourself! But even if it were all true the very fact that you are reflecting upon your situation shows that all is not lost –

LEOPOLD: You're good to me, Marguerite! And please don't call me professor, it sounds so formal! Why aren't you drinking?

(MARGUERITE *has a drink and winces.* LEOPOLD *promptly fills up her glass. Short pause.*)

MARGUERITE: So many people think so highly of you! Doesn't that alone give you strength?

LEOPOLD: On the contrary! I often say to myself how wonderful it was when nobody was interested in me – when nobody expected anything from me and nobody was urging me to do things – I used to browse around the second-hand bookshops – studying modern philosophers at my leisure – spending the nights making notes from their works – taking walks in the parks and meditating –

MARGUERITE: But it's thanks to all that that you are what you are today –

LEOPOLD: That's true, but it's also true that I've taken upon myself a heavier burden than I'm able to bear –

MARGUERITE: Leopold, I believe that you will win through!

LEOPOLD: I have a feeling that my only way out is to accept a term there – somewhere far away from my nearest and dearest – and put my humble trust in a higher will, to give me the chance to atone for my guilt – to lose my apathy and regain my pride – and as a nameless cog in a giant machine to purify myself – thus and only thus – If I manage to drain the bitter cup with dignity – I can get back – perhaps – something of my lost human integrity – renew the hope inside me – reconstitute myself emotionally – open the door to a new life –

MARGUERITE: (*Shouts*) But Leopold!

LEOPOLD: Yes?

MARGUERITE: (*Excitedly*) Don't you see that the punishment is deeply unjust and if you try – however honourably – to turn it into a purifying experience you'd just be agreeing with it

56

and so prostrating yourself before it. And what's more, by giving it this so-called meaning you're hiding from yourself the fact that you're clinging to it as a kind of escape from your life, a way out of your problems. But however far they send you, punishment won't solve what you can't solve yourself! Don't you understand that you've done nothing and so there is nothing to atone! You're innocent!

LEOPOLD: Oh, Marguerite – why didn't I meet you before it was too late?

(LEOPOLD *takes hold of her hands and kisses them.*

MARGUERITE *is embarrassed.* LEOPOLD *holds her hands. She drops her eyes. Long pause*)

MARGUERITE: (*Whispering*) Leopold –

LEOPOLD: Yes –

MARGUERITE: Do you love anybody?

LEOPOLD: Ah, my dear girl, I really don't know if I'm capable of love –

MARGUERITE: Don't tell me that you've never felt anything towards a woman –

LEOPOLD: Nervousness – more with some, less with others –

MARGUERITE: You need love! Mad passionate true love! Didn't you yourself write in *Phenomenology of Responsibility* that a person who doesn't love doesn't exist? Only love will give you the strength to stand up to them!

LEOPOLD: That's easy for you to say, Marguerite, but where would one find it?

(MARGUERITE *takes a quick drink, winces and quietly blurts out.*)

MARGUERITE: With me!

LEOPOLD: What? You?

MARGUERITE: (*Excited*) Yes! You have given me back the meaning to my life, which is to give you the meaning back to yours! I'll save you!

(LEOPOLD *strokes her hair.*)

LEOPOLD: You're wonderful, Marguerite! But I can't allow you to throw your life away on someone as worthless as myself –

MARGUERITE: On the contrary I would be fulfilling my life!

LEOPOLD: Apart from the fact that I'm an old man –

MARGUERITE: That's nonsense! I've made up my mind –

LEOPOLD: If I'd known it would come to this I'd never have told you my problems –

MARGUERITE: Thank goodness you did! I'll give you back strength – courage – self-confidence – joy – appetite for life! I'll bring your failing heart back to life! I know you're capable of love! How else could you have written those things! I'll bring you back to life and at the same time back to philosophy!

(LEOPOLD *takes hold of* MARGUERITE'*s arms and for a moment looks deeply into her eyes and then begins to kiss her rapidly over her face and neck.*)

MARGUERITE: Ah – Leopold – ah – I love you – I love your thoughts and your words – you awoke my love a long time ago without knowing it – without my knowing it – and now I'll awaken love in you!

(*At that moment the doorbell rings.* LEOPOLD *jumps up at once.*)

LEOPOLD: (*Whispering*) Quick – go out on the balcony!

MARGUERITE: (*Whispering*) Why?

LEOPOLD: (*Whispering*) They'll drag you off!

(LEOPOLD *takes her by the hand and hurries her to the balcony door. He opens the door and pushes her on to the balcony and closes the door. He runs into the bedroom leaving the door open. Pause. The doorbell rings again. Pause. Then* LEOPOLD, *grey-faced, emerges from the bedroom wearing a suit and an overcoat and carrying a small military valise. He goes to the front door. Opens it bravely.* FIRST CHAP *and* SECOND CHAP *enter.* LEOPOLD *closes the door behind them.*)

FIRST CHAP: On your own today?

LEOPOLD: (*Bravely*) Gentlemen! Do your duty! I'll get ready!

SECOND CHAP: What's the hurry? It may not come to the worst –

(*The* FIRST CHAP *goes to the balcony door, opens it and says:*)

FIRST CHAP: Come in, my little one –

(MARGUERITE *slowly enters the room.*)

LEOPOLD: Don't you dare touch her! If you drag her off, then –

SECOND CHAP: Then what?

58

LEOPOLD: Then – then –

FIRST CHAP: Don't you worry, there's no need for her to go anywhere. Today there'd be no point –

LEOPOLD: You're right. As you're obviously aware, I'm not going to sign that statement. I'd rather die than give up my own human identity – it's the only thing I've got!

SECOND CHAP: But Professor, why are you carrying on like this? You're not going anywhere –

LEOPOLD: Why not? I've told you quite clearly that I'm not going to sign anything! I'm not guilty!

FIRST CHAP: You don't have to sign anything! Your case has been adjourned indefinitely –

SECOND CHAP: Indefinitely for the time being.

FIRST CHAP: For the time being.

SECOND CHAP: Without signature!

LEOPOLD: What? Adjourned?

FIRST CHAP: That's right. Adjourned!

LEOPOLD: You mean no signature and no *there* either?

SECOND CHAP: For the time being, mind, for the time being –

LEOPOLD: I don't understand what it means – why don't you want my signature any more?

FIRST CHAP: It would be just a formality. Who needs it? It's become pretty clear by now that in your case it would be superfluous –

LEOPOLD: Are you trying to say that I am no longer me?

SECOND CHAP: You said it, not me.

(*Short pause.* LEOPOLD *gazes at the* FIRST *and* SECOND CHAP *and then shouts.*)

LEOPOLD: I don't want an adjournment! I want to go there!
(LEOPOLD *suddenly falls to his knees in front of the* CHAPS *and starts to sob.*)
I'm begging you – I beseech you – I can't go on living like this –

FIRST CHAP: It seems you'll have to –

MARGUERITE: (*Calling to him*) Leopold get up! You're not going to beg them, are you!

LEOPOLD: (*Shouting at* MARGUERITE) Leave me alone! All of you leave me alone!

59

(LEOPOLD *collapses on the floor, banging his fists on it.*
The curtain falls and the music returns.)

SCENE SEVEN

The music is fading and the curtain begins to rise slowly. LEOPOLD
*is alone on the stage. He is sitting on the sofa staring at the front
door. After a longer pause he gets up and goes to the door and looks
through the peep-hole. Then he puts his ear to the door and listens
intently. The lights start to come up in the auditorium and the music
begins to be heard.* LEOPOLD *straightens up slowly, goes to the
footlights and bows. At the same time all the other characters enter
from the various doors and gather round* LEOPOLD *bowing.*
The curtain falls.

END

TEMPTATION

Translated by
George Theiner

For Zdeněk Urbánek

Temptation was first performed at The Other Place,
Stratford-upon-Avon, on 22 April 1987.

The cast was as follows:

DR KOTRLÝ	Ian Barritt
FISTULA	David Bradley
DR LORENCOVÁ	Susan Colverd
MAGGIE	Sally George
VILMA	Julie Legrand
DR NEUWIRTH	Trevor Martin
DEPUTY DIRECTOR	Barrie Rutter
DR FOUSTKA	John Shrapnel
DIRECTOR	Paul Webster

Director	Roger Michell
Set Design	David Roger
Costumes	Alexandra Byrne
Music	Jeremy Sams
Lighting	Rick Fisher

DR HENRY FOUSTKA, *scientist*
FISTULA, *invalid in retirement*
The DIRECTOR
VILMA, *scientist*
The DEPUTY DIRECTOR
MAGGIE, *secretary*
DR LIBUŠE LORENCOVÁ, *scientist*
DR VILÉM KOTRLÝ, *scientist*
DR ALOIS NEUWIRTH, *scientist*
MRS HOUBOVÁ, *Foustka's landlady*
DANCER (*male*)
PETRUŠKA
SECRETARY
FIRST LOVER
SECOND LOVER

Before the curtain rises, in the intervals between the scenes, and during the Intermission, we hear 'cosmic' or 'astral' rock music. It is important for the intervals to be as short as possible – thus the scene changes (despite the variety of settings) carried out as quickly as possible.

We are in one of the rooms of a scientific institute. It combines the functions of an office, consulting-room, library, staff room, and foyer. There are three doors, at the rear, at the front left and front right. At right rear there is a bench, a small table and two chairs; against the rear wall stands a bookcase, a couch, and a white vitrine filled with drugs and various exhibits such as embryos, models of human organs, cult objects of primitive nations, and so on. At left is a desk with a typewriter and papers on it, behind it an office chair, and by the wall a filing cabinet. A large chandelier hangs in the middle of the room. There can also be other objects – a wash-basin, a sun lamp, and so on. The furnishings do not testify to any specific interest, much less any particular personality – rather, they reflect the undefined character of the Institute itself. The whole gives the impression of bureaucratic anonymity, the individual objects having found their way here thanks to the arbitrary decisions of someone in authority rather than because they were actually needed. As the curtain rises, we see LORENCOVÁ, KOTRLÝ *and* NEUWIRTH. LORENCOVÁ *is wearing a white coat and is sitting at the desk, powdering her face, her powder compact propped against the typewriter.* KOTRLÝ, *also in a white coat, is stretched out on the bench, reading a newspaper.* NEUWIRTH, *in ordinary clothes, is standing by the bookcase, his back to the others, examining one of the books.*

A short pause.

LORENCOVÁ: (*Calling*) Maggie . . .

    (MAGGIE *enters, left.*)

MAGGIE: Yes, Doctor.

LORENCOVÁ: Oh, Maggie, would you make me a cup of coffee?

MAGGIE: Yes, of course.

KOTRLÝ: (*Without looking up*) And one for me, please.

NEUWIRTH: (*Without turning round*) And me . . .

MAGGIE: That's three coffees, then?

LORENCOVÁ: Right.

    (MAGGIE *leaves, left. A short pause, then* FOUSTKA *enters quickly by the rear door. He is wearing a black sweater and black trousers, carries a briefcase, is slightly out of breath.*)

FOUSTKA: Hi . . .

KOTRLÝ: (*Lays aside his newspaper*) Hi, Henry.

NEUWIRTH: (*Puts away his book and turns round*) Hi there . . .

(LORENCOVÁ *puts her mirror and powder compact in her coat pocket and crosses to the bench to join* KOTRLÝ, *thus vacating the desk for* FOUSTKA. *He puts down his briefcase and hastily removes some papers from it, watched intently by the others.*)

FOUSTKA: Have they been yet?

KOTRLÝ: Not yet.

LORENCOVÁ: Where's Vilma?

FOUSTKA: Oh, she's slipped out to get some oranges.

(MAGGIE *enters left, carrying three cups of coffee on a small tray; two she places on the table in front of* LORENCOVÁ *and* KOTRLÝ, *handing the third to* NEUWIRTH, *still standing at the back, leaning against the bookcase.*)

LORENCOVÁ: Thanks very much.

(MAGGIE *returns to the door, left.*)

FOUSTKA: Oh, Maggie . . .

MAGGIE: (*Stops*) Yes, Doctor?

FOUSTKA: Sorry about this, but would you mind making another cup of coffee for me?

MAGGIE: Of course not.

FOUSTKA: Thanks.

(MAGGIE *leaves, left.* LORENCOVÁ, KOTRLÝ *and* NEUWIRTH *stir their coffee, at the same time keeping their eyes on* FOUSTKA, *who has taken his place behind the desk and is tidying up various papers and files on it. The lengthy, tense silence is at last broken by* KOTRLÝ.)

KOTRLÝ: (*To* FOUSTKA) Well . . . ?

FOUSTKA: Well what?

KOTRLÝ: How goes it?

FOUSTKA: What, exactly?

(LORENCOVÁ, KOTRLÝ *and* NEUWIRTH *look at one another and smile. A short pause.*)

LORENCOVÁ: Why, your private studies, of course.

FOUSTKA: I don't know what you're talking about.

(LORENCOVÁ, KOTRLÝ *and* NEUWIRTH *look at one another and smile. A short pause.*)

NEUWIRTH: Oh, come off it, Henry – every little child here knows about it.

FOUSTKA: I don't give a damn what little children know about – I am engaged in no other studies than those pertaining directly to my work here at the Institute.

KOTRLÝ: I know what it is – you don't trust us, do you? Can't say I blame you ... in certain matters caution is called for.

NEUWIRTH: Especially if one is engaged on two fronts at once ...

FOUSTKA: (*Giving* NEUWIRTH *a quick glance.*)
And what's that supposed to mean?
(NEUWIRTH *points a conspiratorial finger, first round the room and then at the door, right, indicating the power of the Institute, then he points at the ceiling and at the floor, indicating the power of Heaven and Hell.*)
You're all letting your imaginations run away with you. What about that social tonight – is it still on?

LORENCOVÁ: Naturally ...
(*The* DEPUTY DIRECTOR *enters, right, in his ordinary clothes, accompanied by* PETRUŠKA *who is wearing a white coat. They are holding hands, as they will throughout, which means that* PETRUŠKA, *who will not say a word, will invariably accompany the* DEPUTY. *He, however, pays no attention to her, as if he were merely taking her along as some kind of personal effect or mascot.* LORENCOVÁ, KOTRLÝ *and* NEUWIRTH *rise.*)

KOTRLÝ: Good morning, sir.

DEPUTY: Good morning, friends. Sit down, sit down, please, you know that neither I nor the Director like to stand on ceremony.
(LORENCOVÁ, KOTRLÝ, *and* NEUWIRTH *sit down again. A short pause.*)
So what's the news? Did you all sleep well? Any problems? I don't see Vilma here ...

FOUSTKA: She phoned to say her bus had broken down. But she had managed to find a taxi, she said, so she should be here any minute ...
(*Short pause.*)

DEPUTY: Looking forward to the social, are we? I hope you're all coming?

KOTRLÝ: I'm coming, definitely . . .

LORENCOVÁ: We're all coming.

DEPUTY: Excellent! Personally, I consider our social evenings to be a splendid idea – splendid. Particularly as regards their collectively therapeutic effect. Remarkable how quickly and effectively they help to solve the various interpersonal problems which crop up among us from time to time. Simply thanks to the way we, as individuals, invariably loosen up, while, as a collective, we somehow grow stronger. Wouldn't you say?

KOTRLÝ: Yes, quite, that's exactly how I see it.

DEPUTY: Quite apart from the fact that it would be criminal not to make at least occasional use of such a fine garden.
(*A pause.*)
I came a little earlier on purpose . . .

NEUWIRTH: Is something wrong?

DEPUTY: The Director will tell you himself. All I wanted was to ask you to be sensible – do try to understand him and don't make unnecessary problems for him, he is in a difficult enough position as it is. We all know, after all, that you can't knock down a brick wall with your bare hands – so why make things needlessly difficult for yourselves or for others? I think we can be glad we have such a Director, so that if we lend him support, we're really doing ourselves a favour. Let us bear in mind that he is concerned for our common cause, and that he is no more his own master than the rest of us. It is therefore up to us to display at least a minimum of self-discipline so that neither he, our Institute, nor any one of us should get into hot water. I'm sure you understand and won't expect me to say more than I've already said and am able to say. We're all adults, after all, are we not?

KOTRLÝ: Yes, of course.

DEPUTY: There you are, then. Have you had your soap ration?

FOUSTKA: They're due to bring it today.

DEPUTY: Excellent!

(*The* DIRECTOR *enters, right, wearing a white coat.*
LORENCOVÁ, KOTRLÝ *and* FOUSTKA *rise quickly.*)

KOTRLÝ: Good morning, Director.

DIRECTOR: Hullo there, friends. Do sit down, please, you know that I don't like to stand on ceremony.

DEPUTY: That's just what I told our colleagues, just now, Director.

(LORENCOVÁ, KOTRLÝ *and* FOUSTKA *sit down. The* DIRECTOR *gazes at all those present inquisitively, then goes to* FOUSTKA *and holds out his hand to him.* FOUSTKA *gets up, surprised.*)

DIRECTOR: (*To* FOUSTKA) Did you sleep well?

FOUSTKA: Yes, thank you.

DIRECTOR: Do you have any problems?

FOUSTKA: No, I don't think so ...

(*The* DIRECTOR *squeezes* FOUSTKA's *elbow in a friendly fashion and turns to the others.* FOUSTKA *sits down again.*)

DIRECTOR: Where is Vilma?

DEPUTY: She phoned to say her bus had broken down. But she had managed to find a taxi, she said, so she should be here any minute ...

(MAGGIE *enters, left, with a cup of coffee, which she gives to* FOUSTKA.)

FOUSTKA: Thanks.

MAGGIE: Don't mention it.

(MAGGIE *leaves, left.*)

DIRECTOR: Looking forward to the social, are we?

KOTRLÝ: Very much, Director.

DEPUTY: I have good news for you, friends. The Director has promised to make a short appearance at our social.

LORENCOVÁ: A short one?

DIRECTOR: That'll depend on the circumstances. (*To* FOUSTKA) I hope you'll show up?

FOUSTKA: Yes, of course, Director.

DIRECTOR: Look here, colleagues, no sense in making a meal of it. We all have work to do. So let me get straight to the point: as you probably know, there have lately cropped up complaints that our Institute isn't fulfilling its tasks in keeping with the present situation ...

NEUWIRTH: What situation?

DIRECTOR: Come, come, my friend, let's not beat about the bush. Are we not the people who're supposed to be the first to know things, and the first to take action? But to continue: we're being urged, with increasing insistence, that we go over to the offensive, that is that we should at last somehow try and implement a programme of extensive educational, popular-scientific and individually therapeutic activity ...

DEPUTY: Firmly in the spirit of the scientific *Weltanschauung* ...

DIRECTOR: That, surely, goes without saying?

DEPUTY: I'm sorry, Director, but unfortunately there exists science that is not based on a scientific view of the world ...

DIRECTOR: That is no science where I'm concerned! Now, where was I?

KOTRLÝ: You were saying that we must somehow try and implement ...

DIRECTOR: Yes. In order to counter the isolated but nevertheless alarming expressions of various irrational viewpoints which can be discerned in particular in certain members of our younger generation and which owe their origin to the incorrect ...

The SECRETARY *enters, right. He goes to the* DIRECTOR *and at length whispers in his ear, the* DIRECTOR *nodding all the time and looking serious. The* SECRETARY *stops whispering, the* DIRECTOR *nods for the last time, the* SECRETARY *leaves, right. A short pause.*)

Now, where was I?

KOTRLÝ: You were saying that the irrational viewpoints we have to counter owe their origin ...

DIRECTOR: To the incorrect interpretation of the complexity of natural processes and the historical dynamism of human civilization, some of whose aspects are taken out of context, only to be interpreted, either in the light of pseudo-scientific theories ...

DEPUTY: We have discovered that type-written copies of some of the works of C. J. Jung are circulating among our young people . . .

DIRECTOR: Or in the light of a whole range of mystic prejudices, superstitions, obscure teachings and practices spread by certain charlatans, psychopaths and members of the intelligentsia . . .

(VILMA *comes running in through the rear door. She seems breathless and is carrying a bag of oranges.*)

VILMA: Sorry to be late, Director, but just imagine – the bus I was on . . .

DIRECTOR: Yes, I've heard. Sit down.

(VILMA *sits down on the couch, gesticulating at* FOUSTKA *and obviously trying to convey some message to him.*)

Look here, colleagues, no sense in making a meal of it. We all have work to do. I have already acquainted you with the size of the problem and the tasks it puts in front of us. Now it is up to you. All I want to do is to ask you to be sensible, try and understand and don't make unnecessary problems for me in what is a difficult enough position as it is. We live in modern times, after all.

KOTRLÝ: Yes, that's right, we do.

DIRECTOR: There you are, then. Have you had your soap ration?

FOUSTKA: They're due to bring it today.

(*The* DIRECTOR *goes to* FOUSTKA, *who rises. The* DIRECTOR *puts his hand on* FOUSTKA'*s shoulder and looks him gravely in the face. Then, in a voice charged with emotion, he says:*)

DIRECTOR: I rely on you, Henry . . .

FOUSTKA: You mean, where the soap is concerned?

DIRECTOR: The soap and everything else.

(*Curtain.*)

SCENE TWO

Foustka's flat. A small bachelor's room with a single door at rear right. The walls are covered by bookcases with large quantities of

books; a window, left, and in front of it a large writing desk covered
with papers and yet more books, with a chair behind it and a low
couch to the right. Next to this, a large globe, while on one of the
bookcases hangs a map of the heavens. As the curtain rises,
FOUSTKA *is discovered kneeling in the middle of the room, in a*
dressing-gown, with four burning candles on the floor around him.
He holds a fifth in his left hand, and a piece of chalk in his right,
with which he draws a circle round himself and the candles. Next to
him on the floor lies an open old tome. The room is dimly lit. When
FOUSTKA *has finished drawing his circle he studies the book for a*
time, then shakes his head and murmurs something. There is a knock
on the door. FOUSTKA, *startled, jumps up and calls out.*

FOUSTKA: (*Calling*) Just a moment.

> (FOUSTKA *quickly switches on the light, puts out all the*
> *candles, which he hides behind the desk, removes the book,*
> *looks around and with his foot tries to obliterate the circle he has*
> *drawn on the floor.*)

(*Calling*) Who is it?

HOUBOVÁ: (*Off stage*) It's only me, Doctor.

FOUSTKA: (*Calling*) Just a minute, Mrs Houbová.

(*Clears room.*) Come in.

HOUBOVÁ: Oh dear, the place is full of smoke. You need some
  air.

FOUSTKA: It really doesn't bother me. Anything wrong?

HOUBOVÁ: You have a visitor . . .

FOUSTKA: Have I? Who is it?

HOUBOVÁ: I don't know, he didn't tell me.

FOUSTKA: A stranger, is it?

HOUBOVÁ: Never seen him before.

FOUSTKA: What does he look like?

HOUBOVÁ: I dunno – how should I say, a bit disreputable . . .
  and, worst of all, he . . .

FOUSTKA: What is it, Mrs Houbová?

HOUBOVÁ: I hardly like to say . . .

FOUSTKA: Go on, out with it . . .

HOUBOVÁ: Well, it's just that he . . . smells . . .

FOUSTKA: Is that so? How does he smell?

HOUBOVÁ: Hard to say – like a strong cheese, I guess.

FOUSTKA: Does he really! Never mind, tell him to come in.

(HOUBOVÁ *leaves the room, leaving the door ajar.*)

HOUBOVÁ: (*Off stage*) You're to go in . . .

(FISTULA *enters, a small, slender man with a limp and of dubious appearance. He is holding a paper bag containing a pair of slippers.* HOUBOVÁ *stands in the doorway, following him with her eyes, then shrugs her shoulders at* FOUSTKA *and shuts the door.* FISTULA *grins vacuously.* FOUSTKA *regards him with some astonishment. A pause.*)

FOUSTKA: Good afternoon.

FISTULA: How do you do?

(*A pause.* FISTULA *inspects the room with interest.*)

Very cosy, very cosy indeed. Just as I imagined it. All these learned books . . . a rare globe . . . everything nice and restrained . . . balance in all its glory.

FOUSTKA: Balance? What balance? And anyway, who am I speaking to?

FISTULA: All in good time. May I sit down?

FOUSTKA: Please do . . .

(FISTULA *sits down on the couch, takes off his shoes, removes his slippers from the paper bag and puts them on, replacing them with the shoes and laying the bag on the couch next to him. A pause.*)

FISTULA: I take it I don't have to stress that you should not mention my visit to anyone in your own interest as well as mine?

FOUSTKA: Why should I not mention it?

FISTULA: You'll see soon enough. My name is Fistula. My place of work is immaterial – in any case I don't have a permanent job. Don't have to, you see, being retired as an invalid.

(FISTULA *grins as if he had made a joke.*)

FOUSTKA: I'd hazard a guess that you work in a cheese factory.

(FISTULA *laughs, then grows serious.*)

FOUSTKA: Athlete's foot, my dear sir, or some similar ailment I suffer from, and there's little I can do about it.

(FOUSTKA *perches himself on a corner of the desk and stares at* FISTULA, *with a mixture of curiosity, suspicion and revulsion.*

A longer pause.)

Aren't you going to ask me what it is I want? What is the purpose of my visit?

FOUSTKA: Well, I have not yet given up the hope that you will tell me without being asked.

FISTULA: Of course, there is nothing to prevent me doing just that, and if I haven't done so already, then for a very good reason.

FOUSTKA: What reason is that?

FISTULA: I had rather hoped you'd discover that for yourself.

FOUSTKA: (*Irritated*) How can I when I see you for the first time? And anyway, I have neither the time nor the inclination to play silly guessing games. Unlike you, I happen to have a job and will shortly have to go . . .

FISTULA: I know, to your Institute's social. You have bags of time.

FOUSTKA: How did you know I'm going to our social?

FISTULA: And before I arrived you didn't exactly carry on like a man in a hurry.

FOUSTKA: You can't know anything about what I was doing before you arrived.

FISTULA: Forgive me, but I know far more than you about what I know and what I don't know, and how I know what I know.

(FISTULA *gives another of his asinine grins. A longer pause. Then* FOUSTKA *gets up from the table, walks around it to stand facing* FISTULA, *a serious expression on his face.*)

FOUSTKA: Look here, Mr . . .

FISTULA: Fistula . . .

FOUSTKA: Mr Fistula, I'm asking you straight, and I expect a straight answer: what is it you want?

(*A short pause.*)

FISTULA: Does the name Marbuel mean anything to you? Or Loradiel? Or Lafiel?

(FOUSTKA *looks startled, but recovers his composure, looks at* FISTULA *and shouts.*)

FOUSTKA: Out!

FISTULA: I beg your pardon?

74

FOUSTKA: I said: Out!

FISTULA: How do you mean – out?

FOUSTKA: Leave my flat at once and never show your face here again.

(FISTULA *rubs his hands together contentedly*.)

Did you hear what I said?

FISTULA: Yes, I heard what you said, and I'm delighted at your reaction because it confirms that I have come to the right address . . .

FOUSTKA: I don't understand . . .

FISTULA: Your agitation tells me that you're well aware of the weight of my contacts, which you would hardly be in a position to know unless you had earlier taken an interest in them yourself.

FOUSTKA: Those names mean nothing to me, I have no idea what you're talking about, and the suddenness of my decision to throw you out is due simply to the fact that I have suddenly had enough of you. It is mere coincidence that this happened just as you pronounced those names. Having provided this explanation, perhaps I can repeat what I said earlier without fear that you will put some false interpretation on it: leave my flat at once and never show your face here again!

FISTULA: Your first request – that I leave – I'll naturally comply with, even though not just yet; the second I will not, and you will in time be very grateful to me for it.

FOUSTKA: I'm afraid you didn't understand. Those weren't two mutually independent requests – in fact, they weren't requests at all. It was a command, single and indivisible.

FISTULA: Understood. However, I must add, the alacrity with which you subsequently attributed a different motive to that command, together with the circumstance that, although you had, to use your expression 'had enough of me', you nevertheless found it necessary to acquaint me with this, thus running the risk of postponing my desired departure – all this proves just one thing: that your original fear of me as a representative of those contacts has given way to a fear of me as a possible *agent provocateur*. I therefore have to tell you that this, too, I anticipated. Nay, what is more, if this had not happened I should have found it suspicious and would have had to ask myself if indeed *you* are not an *agent provocateur*. But now let's get down to the matter in hand. There is of course no way I can *prove* to you that I am no *provocateur*; even were I to call forth Ariel himself, here and now, it would not exclude the possibility that I am also trying to provoke you. You thus have only three choices: you can continue to consider me an *agent provocateur* and insist that I leave. Secondly, not to think of me in those terms but instead to trust me. Thirdly, not to make your mind up in this matter just yet and to adopt a waiting posture, which means not to throw me out but on the other hand to say nothing which, if I were an *agent provocateur*, I might be able to use against you. If I may, I'd recommend the third alternative . . .

(FOUSTKA *paces up and down the room in thought, then he sits behind his desk and looks at* FISTULA.)

FOUSTKA: All right, so be it. I should add, though, that in talking to you, I have no need to watch what I say because there is no question that I might think, much less utter, anything that could be used against me.

FISTULA: Splendid! (*He claps enthusiastically.*) I like you. If I were an *agent provocateur*, I'd have to admit that you have passed your first test with flying colours. Your words betray a well-founded caution as well as a sharp intelligence and ready wit, all of which are qualities I can but welcome, for they give me hope that I can rely on you and that we shall work well together . . .

(*A pause.*)

FOUSTKA: Now, listen here, Mr . . .

FISTULA: Fistula . . .

FOUSTKA: Listen here, Mr Fistula, I'd just like to say two things. Firstly: to my mind you talk too much and I wish you'd come more quickly to the point and tell me what brought you here. You have given me no indication, even though I asked you for a straight answer to my straight question. And secondly: it comes as something of a surprise

76

to me to hear that you and I are supposed to be working together on anything. It takes two to tango, you know.

FISTULA: You have just used eighty-seven words to reply to me. Considering their semantic value, that is not exactly a small number, so I would not accuse others of talking too much if I were you.

FOUSTKA: Loquaciousness is well known to be infectious ...

FISTULA: I hope that in time you will also acquire some of my more important skills.

FOUSTKA: What's that? Are you trying to tell me you want to teach me things?

FISTULA: Not just teach ...

FOUSTKA: No? What else, for God's sake?

FISTULA: (Shouts) Leave him out of this!

FOUSTKA: What else do you have in mind, then?

FISTULA: (Smiling) To initiate you ...

(FOUSTKA rises abruptly, bangs the desk with his fist, and shouts.)

FOUSTKA: That's enough! I am a scientist and hold a scientific world view, working in a very responsible position in one of our foremost scientific institutes. If anyone comes to me with ideas that can be defined as an attempt to spread superstition, I shall be forced to act according to my scientific conscience.

(FISTULA stares dumbly at FOUSTKA for a few seconds, then starts to laugh uproariously, hopping about the room as he does so. Suddenly he falls silent, bends down, and slowly draws a circle with his finger on the floor, just as FOUSTKA had done earlier. Then he leaps to his feet and again bursts out laughing. Crossing to the desk, he seizes one of the hidden candles, waves it in the air and, still laughing, places it on the desk. FOUSTKA follows his antics with a glazed look in his eyes. FISTULA suddenly grows serious again, returns to the couch, sits down, and begins to speak in level tones.)

FISTULA: Doctor, I am well acquainted with your views, I know how much your work at the Institute means to you, so please accept my apologies for my stupid joke. In any case, it's high time I abandoned these introductory pleasantries. As your Director was good enough to stress this morning, one of the tasks facing your Institute is to combat certain expressions of irrational mysticism, which still crop up here and there, kept alive by obscure individuals as the remnants of the pre-scientific views of primitive nations and dark historical epochs. As a scientist, you yourself know best that this struggle of yours will be the more effective, the more thorough your knowledge of that which you are struggling against. You have in your possession a remarkable collection of hermetic literature – just about everything worth having, from Agrippa and Nostradamus to Eliphas Levi and Papus – but as you well know, theory is not everything, and I'd seriously doubt that you have never felt the urge to acquaint yourself directly with contemporary magical practice. I come to you as a practitioner with several hundred successful magical evocations behind him, who is prepared to acquaint you with some aspects of his work in order to provide valuable material for your scientific studies. And if you are asking yourself how it is possible for a hermetic to take an interest in the struggle against hermetism, I can give you a frank answer: I find myself in a situation where, without some support, I might come to a sticky end. I therefore offer myself to you as a subject for study, and I shall ask for nothing more in return than that you should, if necessary, testify that I have put myself at the disposal of science and that it would thus be unfair to hold me responsible for spreading something that I am, in actual fact, helping to combat.

(FISTULA *looks gravely at* FOUSTKA, *who is lost in thought for a while. Then he speaks softly.*)

FOUSTKA: I have a suggestion . . .

FISTULA: Yes? I'm listening . . .

FOUSTKA: In order to expedite matters, I'll pretend not to be equipped with a scientific world view, as if I were taking an interest in certain things out of mere curiosity.

FISTULA: Agreed!

(FISTULA *comes forward and holds out his hand to* FOUSTKA.

FOUSTKA *hesitates, then takes his hand and shakes it.*
FOUSTKA *swiftly withdraws his hand again.*)
FOUSTKA: (*Cries out*) Ouch!
(FOUSTKA *rubs his hand and waves it in the air, his face
distorted with pain.*)
Man, your temperature must be fifty below!
FISTULA: (*Laughs*) Not quite . . .
(FOUSTKA *at last recovers and resumes his seat at his desk.*
FISTULA *also sits down, crossing his hands in his lap and
gazing at* FOUSTKA *in a theatrical manner. A longer pause.*)
FOUSTKA: Well?
(*A long pause.*)
What is it?
(*A long pause.*)
Lost your tongue all of a sudden?
FISTULA: I'm waiting . . .
FOUSTKA: Waiting for what?
FISTULA: Your wishes.
FOUSTKA: I don't understand – what wishes?
FISTULA: How can I acquaint you with my knowledge unless
you set me certain tasks – such as you can yourself verify?
FOUSTKA: Oh, I see. What kind of tasks do you have in mind –
roughly?
FISTULA: Come, you know enough about these things . . .
FOUSTKA: Yes, perhaps, but faced with this opportunity of a
practical demonstration . . .
FISTULA: No matter, I'll help you. How about this for an
innocent first step. As far as I know, you fancy a certain
young lady . . .
FOUSTKA: I don't know what you're talking about . . .
FISTULA: Oh come, Doctor, after all that has been said here,
surely you cannot doubt that I might be privy to a secret or
two . . .
FOUSTKA: If you mean the secretary at the Institute, I don't
deny that she is pretty, but that hardly entitles you . . .
FISTULA: What if tonight at that social of yours she were to fall
in love with you? Unexpectedly and, of course, just for a
short time? How about that?

79

(FOUSTKA *paces the room nervously then turns sharply to*
FISTULA.)

FOUSTKA: Please go away!

FISTULA: Who? Me? Why?

FOUSTKA: Yes, you. Go away.

FISTULA: You're not starting that again? Just when I thought
we had come to an understanding.

FOUSTKA: You have insulted me ...

FISTULA: Insulted you? How?

FOUSTKA: Do you think I'm so badly off that I have to use
magic to help me with women? I'm not some dirty old man
conducting experiments on unsuspecting innocent young
virgins for his own sexual gratification. What do you take
me for?

FISTULA: None of us really knows what we're capable of. But
that's not the point. If my well-meant, innocent, spur-of-
the-moment little idea offends you in any way, I naturally
apologize and withdraw it.

FOUSTKA: And another thing: I have a girl-friend and I am
faithful to her.

FISTULA: As she is to you?

FOUSTKA: (*Startled*) Yes. What are you saying?

FISTULA: Forget it ...

FOUSTKA: No, just a minute – you can't get away with hints
like that. I'm not interested in gossip.

FISTULA: Sorry I spoke. If you have decided to turn a blind
eye, that is entirely your business ...

(FISTULA *removes his shoes from the paper bag and slowly puts
them on.* FOUSTKA *looks on in some embarrassment. A pause.*)

FOUSTKA: Are you leaving?

(*A pause.*)

I just let off a little steam ...

(*A pause.* FISTULA *has changed his footwear, put his slippers
back in the paper bag, and is slowly making his way to the
door.*)

So what's to become of it?

FISTULA: (*Stops and turns*) What's to become of what?

FOUSTKA: Our agreement, I mean.

FISTULA: Well..?
FOUSTKA: Is it still on?
FISTULA: That is entirely up to you.
(FISTULA *grins. The curtain falls.*)

SCENE THREE

The garden of the Institute. It is night, and the garden is illuminated with Chinese lanterns suspended from wires among the trees. In the middle there is a small summer-house, behind it a space serving as a dance-floor. Front left, a garden bench, right, a garden table with various drinks and glasses. All around are trees and shrubs, which combine with the dim light to screen the dancers from view; figures moving about the garden are also seen only dimly. Only the action at front of the stage can be clearly seen. As the curtain rises, the music grows softer and changes in character: we hear commercial dance music, which will accompany the entire scene. Two LOVERS are sitting in the summer-house; they will remain there throughout the scene, gently embracing, stroking and kissing each other and whispering in each other's ear, oblivious to their surroundings. The DEPUTY is dancing with PETRUŠKA and KOTRLÝ with LORENCOVÁ; apart from these two couples, the DIRECTOR and VILMA move around the dance-floor separately. FOUSTKA is standing by the refreshments table, pouring two drinks; MAGGIE is sitting on the bench. Everyone is in evening dress, the ladies in formal gowns. As the scene opens, FOUSTKA is explaining something to MAGGIE, who listens in rapt silence. As he speaks, FOUSTKA finishes pouring the drinks and walks slowly over to MAGGIE, carrying the two glasses.

FOUSTKA: We have to realize that out of the infinite number of possible velocities, the expansion of the universe chose precisely the one which gave rise to the universe as we know it, that is, with sufficient time and other prerequisites for the formation of solid bodies, so that life could exist on them – or at least on one of them! Isn't that a remarkable coincidence?

MAGGIE: Yes, quite remarkable.

(FOUSTKA *has now reached* MAGGIE *and hands her one of the glasses, sits down next to her, and they both sip their drink.*)

FOUSTKA: It is, isn't it. And if you delve further, you'll discover that you owe your existence to such an incredible number of equally incredible coincidences that it exceeds all conceivable ratios of probability. Surely all this cannot be an accident; behind it must be concealed some more profound intention of existence, of the world and of nature, willing you, me to exist, willing life as such to exist, and at its apex, as far as it is given to us at present to know, the human spirit capable of reflecting on all this. Does it not strike you as if the cosmos had actually determined to see itself one day through our eyes and to put the questions which we are now putting, with our lips?

MAGGIE: Oh yes, that's exactly how it strikes me.

(VILMA, *who has left the dance-floor, appears at the table, and pours herself a drink.*)

VILMA: Having a good time, you two?

FOUSTKA: Maggie and I have been discussing some philosophical questions . . .

VILMA: Oh, in that case, don't let me disturb you . . .

(VILMA, *glass in hand, disappears; a little later she can again be seen dancing solo on the dance-floor.*)

FOUSTKA: And another thing: modern biology has long been aware that while the law of the survival of the fittest and similar discoveries explain a great deal, they fail altogether to explain why life should exist in the first place, life with the endless variety of its manifestations, life, which seems to be here only because existence wishes to display its own power. But for whose sake, though? Have you ever given any thought to this?

MAGGIE: Not quite like that, I must admit. But now, I guess I'll think about it always . . . you know how to put it so nicely.

(NEUWIRTH *appears from the right, comes up to the bench, and bows to* MAGGIE.)

NEUWIRTH: May I have the pleasure?

MAGGIE: (*Embarrassed*) Why . . . yes . . . of course . . .

(MAGGIE *gives* FOUSTKA *a questioning, unhappy look, then gets up.*)

FOUSTKA: You'll come back, won't you?

MAGGIE: But of course! It's all so terribly interesting . . .

(NEUWIRTH *offers his arm to* MAGGIE *and the two disappear, to be seen again a little later, dancing.* FOUSTKA, *lost in thought, sips his drink. The* DIRECTOR, *who has left the dance-floor, appears from behind a shrub to the left of the bench.*)

DIRECTOR: A splendid evening, isn't it?

(FOUSTKA, *startled, gets up.*)

FOUSTKA: Why, yes . . . we've been lucky in the weather . . .

DIRECTOR: Do sit down. May I join you?

FOUSTKA: Yes, please do . . .

(*They both sit down on the bench. A slight pause. Then the* DIRECTOR *takes* FOUSTKA *by the hand and looks closely into his eyes.*)

DIRECTOR: Henry . . .

FOUSTKA: Yes . . .?

DIRECTOR: Tell me frankly – what do you think of me?

FOUSTKA: What . . . do I think . . .? Well, how should I say, I think that everyone at the Institute is glad that you are in charge . . .

DIRECTOR: No, you don't understand. What I want to know is what you personally think of me – as a man . . . or, to put it more accurately, what are your feelings towards me?

FOUSTKA: I feel great respect for you . . .

DIRECTOR: Respect. Is that all?

FOUSTKA: Well . . . how to say it . . . it's very difficult . . .

(*The* DEPUTY DIRECTOR *appears on the right, accompanied by* PETRUŠKA, *having left the dance-floor; they are holding hands. The* DIRECTOR *sees them and lets go of* FOUSTKA's *hand, to* FOUSTKA's *evident relief.*)

DEPUTY: So here you are, Director. We've been looking for you . . .

DIRECTOR: Anything wrong?

(*Taking advantage of the situation,* FOUSTKA *gets up and quickly walks away.*)

DEPUTY: Nothing in particular. It's only that Petruška here wants to ask you something but is too shy to say so . . .

DIRECTOR: Ask me what?

DEPUTY: She wants to ask you whether you would dance with her.

DIRECTOR: I'm afraid I don't know how to lead, I'd only trample her dress. But there are so many better dancers here . . .

DEPUTY: In that case, would you at least accept our invitation and accompany us to the pond, where colleague Kotrlý has built a delightful underwater light display.

(*The* DIRECTOR *gets up, irritated, and goes off to the right with the* DEPUTY *and* PETRUŠKA. *At the same time,* KOTRLÝ *and* LORENCOVÁ *appear on the left, having left the dance-floor. They cross to the refreshments table.*)

KOTRLÝ: Have you seen my underwater light display yet?

LORENCOVÁ: You're doing it all wrong, Willy.

KOTRLÝ: What am I doing wrong?

(*They have reached the table and* KOTRLÝ *pours two drinks, handing one to* LORENCOVÁ. *They both sip their drinks.*)

LORENCOVÁ: You're crawling so abjectly that before long those two idiots will get fed up with you and you'll be the laughing stock of the Institute. Apart from which, everyone will want to see you come a cropper.

KOTRLÝ: Maybe I *am* doing it all wrong, but that's still better than pretending I'm not interested and at the same time telling 'em everything . . .

LORENCOVÁ: I take it you're referring to Neuwirth?

KOTRLÝ: Who else? Who was it first started blabbing about Foustka's dabbling in magic? If they get to hear of it, Neuwirth will be to blame.

LORENCOVÁ: But we all talked about it! You're being unfair to Neuwirth; your only excuse is that you're jealous . . .

KOTRLÝ: I might have known you'd take his side!

LORENCOVÁ: Look, don't start that again!

KOTRLÝ: Líba, give me your word there is nothing between you.

LORENCOVÁ: I give you my word. How about another dance?

(KOTRLÝ *and* LORENCOVÁ *put down their glasses and go off to the right; a little later they can be seen dancing in the background.* NEUWIRTH *and* MAGGIE *appear from the left.* MAGGIE *sits down on the bench,* NEUWIRTH *remains standing. From behind the bench* FOUSTKA *pops up round a shrub and sits down next to* MAGGIE.)

NEUWIRTH: Oh, well, let me not disturb you . . .
(NEUWIRTH *goes off, to be seen a little later dancing with* LORENCOVÁ, *whom he has taken away from* KOTRLÝ. *Also on the dance-floor can now be seen the* DEPUTY *dancing with* PETRUŠKA, *and the* DIRECTOR, *dancing on his own. A short pause.*)

MAGGIE: Go on, talk some more! Each word of yours seems to open my eyes . . . I can't understand how I could have been so blind – so superficial . . .

FOUSTKA: I'd just like to start, if I may, from a completely different angle. Have you ever thought that we would be quite unable to understand even the most simple moral action which is not motivated by self-interest, that in fact it would appear to be quite absurd, if we did not admit to ourselves that somewhere within it there is concealed the prerequisite of something higher, some absolute, omniscient and infinitely just moral authority, through which and in which all our actions gain a mysterious worth and through which each and every one of us constantly touches eternity?

MAGGIE: Yes, yes, that's exactly how I've always felt it to be. Only I was never able to say it, let alone put it into such splendid words.

FOUSTKA: There you are! All the more tragic, then, that modern man has chosen to deny everything that is larger than him, to deride the very notion that there might be something higher and that his life and the world at large could possibly have some higher meaning. Having set himself up as the highest authority, he now watches in horror where the world is heading.

MAGGIE: Isn't it all so clear and simple! I do admire the way you look at these things in such a . . . well, I mean, it's all

85

so original . . . so different from the way people usually talk
about them . . . and you take it all so seriously. I don't
think I'll ever forget this evening. I feel as if, in your
company, I'm becoming a new person every minute –
please don't be annoyed that I'm being so frank, but you
seem to emanate a . . . I don't understand how I could have
been indifferent to you all this time . . . in a word, I've
never felt anything like this before.

(KOTRLÝ *appears from the right, approaches the bench, and
bows to* MAGGIE.)

KOTRLÝ: May I have the pleasure?

MAGGIE: Oh, I'm sorry, but . . .

KOTRLÝ: Oh, come on, Maggie – we haven't danced together
yet.

(MAGGIE *gives* FOUSTKA *an unhappy look; he just shrugs his
shoulders;* MAGGIE *gets up.*)

MAGGIE: (*To* FOUSTKA) You'll wait here for me, won't you?

FOUSTKA: Yes, of course.

(KOTRLÝ *offers his arm to* MAGGIE *and the two disappear, to
be seen again a little later, dancing.* FOUSTKA, *lost in thought,
sips his drink. The* DIRECTOR, *who has left the dance-floor,
appears from behind a shrub to the left of the bench.*)

DIRECTOR: Alone again, are you?

(FOUSTKA, *startled, gets up.*)

Sit down, Henry, sit down . . .

(FOUSTKA *resumes his seat. The* DIRECTOR *again takes
FOUSTKA by the hand and looks closely into his eyes.*)

DIRECTOR: Henry . . . ?

FOUSTKA: Yes?

DIRECTOR: Would you like to be my deputy?

FOUSTKA: Your deputy? Me?

DIRECTOR: I could swing it . . .

FOUSTKA: But you already have a deputy . . .

DIRECTOR: If only you knew how I loathe that shit.

(*The* SECRETARY *enters, right. He goes to the* DIRECTOR *and
whispers at length in his ear, the* DIRECTOR *nodding all the
time and looking serious. The* SECRETARY *stops whispering,
the* DIRECTOR *nods for the last time, the* SECRETARY *leaves,*

right. The DIRECTOR, *who has clung to* FOUSTKA's *hand all this time, now turns to* FOUSTKA *and stares long and hard into his eyes.)*

DIRECTOR: Henry . . .

FOUSTKA: Yes?

DIRECTOR: How about coming back to my place when this is over? Or we needn't stay till the end, simply disappear. I have some home-made cherry brandy and I'd show you my collection of miniatures, and we could have a good chat, undisturbed. If it got late, and you didn't feel like making your way home, you could stay the night. You know that I live all alone, and it's only a stone's throw from the Institute, so you'd find it easy in the morning . . . What do you say?

FOUSTKA: Thank you very much, I appreciate your invitation, but you see, I've already promised . . .

DIRECTOR: Who? Vilma?

(FOUSTKA nods. The DIRECTOR again looks him straight in the eye, then irritably pushes his hand away, jumps up, crosses to the refreshments table, pours himself a drink and downs it in a single gulp. FOUSTKA remains sitting on the bench, not quite knowing what to do. The DEPUTY and PETRUŠKA, who have left the dance-floor, appear on the left; they are holding hands and make straight for the DIRECTOR.)

DEPUTY: So here you are, Director. We've been looking for you . . .

DIRECTOR: Anything wrong?

DEPUTY: Nothing in particular. Petruška and I just wanted to ask you what you're doing after this is over. We should be honoured if you'd accept our invitation for a nightcap. Of course, you can sleep at our place, should you wish . . .

DIRECTOR: No, I'm sorry, I am very tired. I have to go home . . .

(The DIRECTOR marches off to the right. The DEPUTY follows him with his eyes, then disappears, left, abashed and with PETRUŠKA in tow. A little later they can be seen dancing in the background. At the same time, NEUWIRTH and LORENCOVÁ appear, right, having left the dance-floor.)

NEUWIRTH: I've seen a lot, but the sight of an educated man trying to curry favour with his cretinous bosses with tricks such as those coloured electric bulbs in the bloody pond – that really takes the biscuit!

(NEUWIRTH *pours two drinks, handing one to* LORENCOVÁ. *They both sip their drinks.*)

LORENCOVÁ: I'd say it's better to curry favour with those coloured bulbs in the pond than to pretend you're not interested and at the same time tell 'em everything . . .

NEUWIRTH: I might have known you'd take his side!

LORENCOVÁ: Look, don't start that again!

NEUWIRTH: Líba, give me your word there is nothing between you.

LORENCOVÁ: I give you my word. How about another dance?

(NEUWIRTH *and* LORENCOVÁ *put down their glasses and go off to the left; a little later they can be seen dancing in the background.* KOTRLÝ *and* MAGGIE *appear from the right.* MAGGIE *sits down on the bench next to* FOUSTKA. KOTRLÝ *remains standing. An embarrassed pause.*)

KOTRLÝ: Oh, well, don't let me disturb you . . .

(KOTRLÝ *goes off, to be seen a little later dancing with* LORENCOVÁ, *whom he has taken away from* NEUWIRTH.)

FOUSTKA: When man drives God out of his heart, he makes way for the Devil. What else is this contemporary world of ours, with its blind, power-crazed rulers and its blind, powerless subjects, what else is the catastrophe that is being prepared under the banner of science – with us as its grotesque flag-bearers – what else is it other than the work of the Devil? It is well known that the Devil is a master of disguise. Can you imagine a more ingenious disguise than that offered him by our modern lack of faith? No doubt he finds he can work best where people have stopped believing in him. Forgive me for speaking so frankly, Maggie, but I cannot hold it back any longer. But who else can I confide in but you?

(MAGGIE *throws her glass into the bushes, grasps both* FOUSTKA'*s hands, and cries:*)

MAGGIE: I love you!

FOUSTKA: No!

MAGGIE: Yes, and I'll go on loving you till the day I die.

FOUSTKA: You unhappy girl! With me you're doomed.

MAGGIE: Rather doomed with you and in truth, than to live
without you and live a lie.

(MAGGIE *embraces* FOUSTKA *and begins to kiss him
passionately,* VILMA *appears by the side of the refreshments
table, having left the dance-floor. For a while she gazes at the
kissing couple, then she says in an icy voice.*)

VILMA: Having a good time?

(FOUSTKA *and* MAGGIE *jump apart and look at* VILMA *in
consternation. The curtain falls.*)

SCENE FOUR

VILMA's *flat. It is a comfortable place, furnished like a lady's
boudoir, full of antique furniture. A door at rear; on the left a large
bed with a canopy; on the right, two armchairs, a large Venetian
mirror, and a dressing-table with a multitude of jars and perfume
bottles. The room is full of scattered knick-knacks and woman's
clothes, only* FOUSTKA's *evening dress lies neatly folded by the bed.
Evident care has been taken to match the colours in the apartment,
with pink and violet predominating. As the curtain rises,* FOUSTKA
is sitting in his underpants on the edge of the bed, VILMA, *wearing a
lace negligée, by the dressing-table, facing the mirror and with her
back to* FOUSTKA. *She is combing her hair. A short pause.*

FOUSTKA: When was he here last?

VILMA: Who?

FOUSTKA: Oh, don't ask such stupid questions!

VILMA: You mean that dancer? About a week ago . . .

FOUSTKA: And you let him in?

VILMA: He just brought me a bunch of violets. I told him I
didn't have time, that I was meeting you . . .

FOUSTKA: I asked whether you let him in.

VILMA: I don't remember . . . maybe he did come in for a
while . . .

FOUSTKA: So you kissed each other.

89

VILMA: I kissed him on the cheek when he gave me those violets. That's all.

FOUSTKA: Vilma, be so kind as not to treat me like an idiot. A kiss on the cheek! Once you let him in I'm sure he'd expect a little more than that. At the very least he'd want to dance with you.

VILMA: Henry, please leave it alone. Can't you find something more interesting to talk about?

FOUSTKA: Did he or didn't he?

VILMA: All right, if you must know, he did. And that's all I'm going to say. I refuse to discuss this any longer because it's undignified, offensive and ridiculous. As if you didn't know that I love you and that no dancer can pose a threat to you. So please no more of this interrogation. After all, I don't give *you* the third degree – even though I have more reason to than you.

FOUSTKA: So you refuse to answer? That, of course, speaks for itself.

VILMA: I have told you again and again that he means nothing to me, I don't go out of my way to see him, I don't dance with him. What more am I supposed to do, damn it?

FOUSTKA: He's always flitting around you, flattering you, wanting to dance with you – and you lap it up! If you didn't, you'd have put an end to it long ago.

VILMA: All right. I don't deny his attentions flatter me. Any woman would feel the same. I'm touched by his persistence, the way he refuses to give up even though he knows he hasn't got a chance. Would you be capable of turning up here at night, from heaven knows where, just to hand me a bunch of violets – at the same time knowing it was hopeless?

FOUSTKA: He persists because you deny him in a way that kindles his hope, and you resist him in a fashion that fuels his desire. If only you'd slam the door on those hopes of his, he'd never show his face here again. But you won't do that because it amuses you to play cat-and-mouse with him. You whore!

VILMA: You have obviously made up your mind to insult me.

FOUSTKA: For how long did you dance with him?

VILMA: Now that's really enough, Henry. You're becoming a bore. I've known for a long time that you're something of an eccentric, but I'd never have guessed you could be so vicious. You seem to be in the grip of a pathological jealousy. And you're being insensitive, tactless, petty-minded and vengeful to boot! If at least you had a real reason...

FOUSTKA: So you intend to go on whoring?

VILMA: You have no right to speak to me like this! You spent the whole evening dancing attendance on that stupid girl, embarrassing everybody in sight, while I trotted around like an idiot – and now you start reproaching *me*. Me! You do as you bloody well please and I have to suffer in silence – and we end up with you making a scene on account of some stupid dancer. How ridiculous can you get! Do you realize how unjust it all is? Do you understand how selfish and cruel you've become?

FOUSTKA: First of all, I don't dance attendance on anybody, and I won't have you referring to Maggie as 'that stupid girl'; secondly, we're not talking about me now, we're talking about you, so kindly don't try to change the subject. Sometimes it seems to me that there is some monstrous plot behind all this: you first of all arouse feelings in me which I had thought long since dead, and then – having robbed me of my ability to be objective about things – you spin your treacherous web around my heart, the more vile since it is woven out of a large number of threads of seemingly innocent dancing visits. Well, I'm not going to let myself be stretched on this rack any longer. I'm going to do something to myself ... or him ... or you – or all of us!

(VILMA *lays down her comb, rises, and advances smilingly towards* FOUSTKA, *clapping her hands as she does so.*
FOUSTKA *now also smiles and goes forward to meet her.*)

VILMA: Your performance gets better every day.

FOUSTKA: Well, you're pretty good yourself ...

(FOUSTKA *and* VILMA *embrace each other tenderly, kiss, then walk slowly towards the bed. They sit up in it next to each*

*other, lean back against the pillows, and cover their legs with a
duvet.* FOUSTKA *lights a cigarette for both of them. A longish
pause is broken by* VILMA.)

VILMA: Tell me, Henry –

FOUSTKA: Yes?

VILMA: Don't you get tired of it at times?

FOUSTKA: Tired of what?

VILMA: Of me making you take part in these games?

FOUSTKA: Well, truth to tell, it did irritate me at first.

VILMA: And now?

FOUSTKA: Now it's beginning to scare me.

VILMA: *Scare* you? Why is that?

FOUSTKA: It seems to me I'm beginning to take it a bit
seriously.

VILMA: (*Cries out*) Henry! You're not really getting jealous, are
you? That's wonderful. I never thought such a success
possible. That you would show anything but a *feigned*
jealousy...

FOUSTKA: Sorry, but I can't share your enthusiasm...

VILMA: I don't see what it is you're afraid of.

FOUSTKA: Of myself.

VILMA: Oh, come on.

FOUSTKA: No, don't underestimate it, Vilma. Something is
going on inside me – I feel I'd be capable of doing things
that were always alien to me. As if something that had lain
hidden deep inside me was suddenly floating to the surface.

VILMA: You do exaggerate, Henry. For once you feel a little
healthy jealousy, and you're panicking. There's nothing the
matter with you; maybe you're a little disconcerted by the
goings on at the Institute, after tonight's unfortunate
encounter with the Director – no, don't deny it, it *is*
worrying you even if you don't want to admit it – but it's
getting at you sub-consciously, and you then see bogeys
where there aren't any.

FOUSTKA: If only it were as simple as that...

(*A pause.*)

VILMA: You think he'll destroy you?

FOUSTKA: He'll certainly try. Question is, does he have the

necessary power?

VILMA: He has as much power as he wants – certainly where we're concerned.

FOUSTKA: But there are other kinds of power than that which he happens to wield.

(VILMA *jumps up in bed, startled, and kneels on a pillow facing* FOUSTKA.)

VILMA: You're serious, aren't you?

FOUSTKA: Yes.

VILMA: Now you are scaring *me*. Please promise me you won't dabble in anything of that sort.

FOUSTKA: What if I don't promise?

VILMA: I told you that invalid would bring us nothing but trouble. He's got you all confused. Don't tell me you would really take him up on his offer?

FOUSTKA: Well, why not?

VILMA: That's dreadful!

FOUSTKA: At least you can see I wasn't just letting off steam.

(*The doorbell rings,* VILMA *cries out, and quickly hides under the bedclothes.* FOUSTKA *smiles, gets up just as he is, in his underpants, crosses to the door and opens it. The* DANCER *is standing in the doorway, with a bunch of violets hidden behind his back.*)

DANCER: Good evening. Is Vilma in?

FOUSTKA: Why?

DANCER: (*Shows him the flowers*) I just wanted to give her something . . .

FOUSTKA: (*Calls in the direction of the bed*) Vilma, you've got a visitor . . .

(VILMA *climbs out of bed, a little confused; she can't find anything to put on, so she finally goes to the door in her negligée.* FOUSTKA *moves aside but stays where he is.*)

VILMA: Thank you . . .

DANCER: Well, I'll be off again . . . sorry if I disturbed you . . .

VILMA: Bye-bye then.

(*The* DANCER *leaves;* VILMA *shuts the door, smiles uncertainly at* FOUSTKA, *lays the violets down on a table, comes up to* FOUSTKA *and kisses him gently on the forehead, cheeks and* mouth. FOUSTKA *stands as if rooted to the spot, gazing coldly in front of him.*)

I love you.

(FOUSTKA *does not bat an eyelid, as* VILMA *goes on kissing him. Then suddenly* FOUSTKA *slaps her brutally across the face;* VILMA *falls to the ground;* FOUSTKA *kicks her. The curtain falls.*)

SCENE FIVE

The same room in the Institute as that in which Scene One took place. As the curtain rises the room is empty, but then FOUSTKA *and* VILMA *enter by the rear door.* FOUSTKA *is still wearing the evening clothes he had on the previous night;* VILMA *a white coat. She has a black eye. They both seem happy.*

VILMA: Don't tell me we're the first!

FOUSTKA: Have you noticed that you only arrive on time when I sleep at your place?

VILMA: You do exaggerate . . .

(FOUSTKA *sits down at the desk and arranges the papers on it:* VILMA *sits down on the couch.*)

(*Calls out*) Maggie . . .

(MAGGIE *enters by the door left, dressed in office clothes. When she catches sight of* FOUSTKA *she stops and lowers her eyes.*)

Would you make us two coffees? Strong ones, if possible.

MAGGIE: Yes, yes, of course . . .

(MAGGIE *returns nervously to the door, stealing a glance at* FOUSTKA *as she goes. He looks up from his papers and gives her a jovial smile.*)

FOUSTKA: Did you sleep well?

MAGGIE: (*Stammering*) Yes, thank you, well . . . why no, not really . . . I had so much to think about . . .

(MAGGIE *leaves the room in obvious confusion.*)

VILMA: I'd say, Henry, that you really managed to turn the poor girl's head last night.

FOUSTKA: Oh, she'll get over it.

(*A pause.*)

VILMA: Henry . . .

FOUSTKA: Yes, darling?

VILMA: It was good last night, wasn't it? I can't remember when we made love so beautifully . . .

FOUSTKA: Mmm.

(*LORENCOVÁ enters by the rear door, in ordinary clothes, accompanied by KOTRLÝ, also in civvies, and NEUWIRTH wearing a white coat.*)

KOTRLÝ: Oh, you're here already.

VILMA: Surprised, aren't you?

(*LORENCOVÁ and KOTRLÝ take their places on the bench, NEUWIRTH leans against the bookcase.*)

LORENCOVÁ: (*Noticing VILMA's black eye*) What on earth is that?

VILMA: Unbridled passion, what else?

(*MAGGIE enters, left, carrying two cups of coffee on a tray. She hands one to VILMA and places the other with a shaking hand in front of FOUSTKA.*)

FOUSTKA: Thank you.

LORENCOVÁ: How about us, Maggie . . .

MAGGIE: Yes, of course, Doctor . . .

(*MAGGIE departs quickly, left. The DEPUTY enters, right, in a white coat and with PETRUŠKA in a dress; they are holding hands. The others get up.*)

KOTRLÝ: Good morning, sir.

DEPUTY: Good morning, friends. Sit down, sit down. I see that today you're all here early. Splendid, though today of all days I'd hardly have expected it.

(*They all sit down again.*)

Well, I believe we had a most successful evening last night. You all deserve thanks for that. Of course, special recognition goes to Kotrlý here for his underwater lighting effects.

KOTRLÝ: Oh, that was nothing . . .

DEPUTY: No point, friends, in beating about the bush . . .

NEUWIRTH: Anything wrong?

DEPUTY: The Director will tell you himself. All I wanted was to ask you to see things as they are, and to try and help us as we try to help you, and in particular that you keep a cool head at this difficult juncture – a cool head, a passionate heart and clean hands. There are moments in life when people either show their mettle – in which case they have nothing to fear – or they don't measure up – and then they have only themselves to thank for the unnecessary difficulties they create for themselves. But you're all educated people, and so I don't have to draw you a picture, do I? Now, who'll volunteer to clear up the garden?

KOTRLÝ: I will, if you like. I have to remove all those bulbs anyway.

DEPUTY: Splendid.

(*The* DIRECTOR *enters, right, in ordinary clothes. They all get up again.*)

KOTRLÝ: Good morning, Director.

DIRECTOR: Good morning, friends. I see that today you're all here early. Splendid, though today of all days I'd hardly have expected it, and yet it is particularly important this morning . . .

DEPUTY: That's just what I told our colleagues just now, Director.

(*They all sit down again. The* DIRECTOR *looks at them for a while, studying their faces, then he goes to* KOTRLÝ *and holds out his hand to him.* KOTRLÝ *gets up, surprised.*)

DIRECTOR: (*To* KOTRLÝ) Did you sleep well?

KOTRLÝ: Yes, thank you.

DIRECTOR: Do you have any problems?

KOTRLÝ: No, I don't think so . . .

(*The* DIRECTOR *squeezes* KOTRLÝ's *elbow in a friendly fashion and turns to the others.* KOTRLÝ *sits down again.*)

DIRECTOR: Look here, colleagues, no sense in making a meal of it . . .

NEUWIRTH: Anything wrong?

DIRECTOR: As we all know, our Institute is a kind of lighthouse of true knowledge, indeed, I might say it is – in its role of a vigilant guardian of the very scientific nature of science – something like the avant-garde of progress. One could say, to put it in a nutshell: what we think today, others will live tomorrow!

96

DEPUTY: Yes, Director, I have already reminded our colleagues of the responsibility this role places on all of us . . .

DIRECTOR: But why am I telling you all this . . . Something serious has happened.

(*The* SECRETARY *enters, right. He goes to the* DIRECTOR *and whispers at length in his ear, the* DIRECTOR *nodding all the time and looking serious. The* SECRETARY *stops whispering, the* DIRECTOR *nods for the last time and resumes speaking; the* SECRETARY *leaves, right.*)

But why am I telling you all this. Something serious has happened.

(MAGGIE *enters, left, carrying three cups of coffee on a small tray; two she places on the table in front of* LORENCOVÁ *and* KOTRLÝ, *handing the third to* NEUWIRTH. *Then she crosses to the same door, left.*)

But why am I telling you all this . . . Something serious has happened.

(MAGGIE *stops in the doorway, looks at the* DIRECTOR, *then at* FOUSTKA, *and then stays by the door, listening.*)

NEUWIRTH: Anything wrong?

DEPUTY: (*To* NEUWIRTH) Please don't interrupt the Director. He's just about to tell us . . .

DIRECTOR: Something serious has happened. The virus has lodged where one would least have expected it, but where, at the same time, it can cause the most damage – that is, in the very centre of the anti-virus campaign – or, to stay with the metaphor – in the central store of antibiotics.

(*All those present look at one another in consternation.* VILMA *and* FOUSTKA *exchange glances showing that they know what it is all about;* FOUSTKA *nervously tries to find a cigarette, takes one out and lights it.*)

KOTRLÝ: Are you telling us, Director, that right here – someone – that one of us . . .

DIRECTOR: Yes, that's exactly what I am telling you, filled as I am with deep sorrow, shame and indignation. We have here in our midst, in this scientific institute – I underline the word scientific – someone who for a long time now and of course in complete secrecy, which only goes to show his two-faced character, has been engaged in various so-called hermetic practices, beginning with astrology, through alchemy all the way to magic, seeking in these murky waters the hidden treasure of allegedly higher – in other words, pre-scientific – learning.

KOTRLÝ: Does that mean he believes in ghosts?

DIRECTOR: Not only that – he has been trying to combine theory with practice. We have ascertained that he has established contact . . .

LORENCOVÁ: With spirits?

DIRECTOR: That's enough! Kindly do not jest about matters that are a blot on the work of our Institute, a direct attack on its reputation and thus a blow below the belt to all of us, and in particular to me who carries the responsibility for our scientific credibility. This is a very grave and sad matter, my friends, and it is up to us all to find an honourable solution. Where was I?

DEPUTY: You were speaking about those contacts . . .

DIRECTOR: Oh yes. Recently, as we have ascertained, he made contact with a certain element from the murky world of pseudo-science, common criminality and moral degeneration, who is suspected of spreading superstition and fooling credulous people with his tricks, and who moreover dabbles in such poisonous things as satanism, black magic, and similar heinous practices. That then is how things stand, and I throw the meeting open to discussion. Any questions?

(*A heavy pause. Then* KOTRLÝ *speaks out softly.*)

KOTRLÝ: May we know the name of this . . . colleague?

DIRECTOR: (*To the* DEPUTY) Tell them.

DEPUTY: I can scarcely bring myself to say it, but name him I must. Very well then – it is Dr Foustka.

(*A heavy pause.*)

DIRECTOR: Yes; anyone else wish to speak?

MAGGIE: (*Diffidently*) Yes, I do . . .

FOUSTKA: (*To* MAGGIE) No – please stay out of this!

DIRECTOR: This concerns us all without exception.

MAGGIE: Forgive me, Director, I am no scientist and I don't

know how to put it – but this simply can't be true! Dr Foustka is a wise and honourable man ... I know he is ... he worries about things which by rights we all should be worrying about – he tries to think things out for himself ... to get to the bottom of things ... all the important things, that is, the sources of morality, the order of the universe ... All the rest – all this talk about those contacts ... I simply don't believe it. I'm sure it's all just gossip, put about by malicious people who wish to harm him. (*There follows a deathly silence.* FOUSTKA *is obviously desperately unhappy at* MAGGIE'*s intervention. The* DIRECTOR *turns to the* DEPUTY.)

DIRECTOR: (*To the* DEPUTY) When we finish here, please arrange for her immediate dismissal. Our Institute really cannot now afford the luxury of employing secretaries who accuse the management of lying.

DEPUTY: I'll see to it, Director.

DIRECTOR: (*To* MAGGIE) You can go and pack your things ...

FOUSTKA: (*Softly, to* MAGGIE) What possessed you? So needlessly to ruin your life – who'll give you a job after this?

MAGGIE: I want to suffer with you!

FOUSTKA: Excuse me, Director, would it not be more sensible to send her for treatment? You can see she doesn't know what she is saying.

DIRECTOR: Psychiatric hospitals are not a cloakroom where one deposits girls whom one first confuses with high-falutin ideas and then wants to get rid of ...

MAGGIE: Are you renouncing me, Henry? And renouncing everything you told me last night?

FOUSTKA: (*Angrily, through clenched teeth*) Be quiet, do you hear?

(MAGGIE *bursts into tears and runs out, left. An embarrassed pause.*)

VILMA: (*To* FOUSTKA) If she does something foolish, it'll be your fault.

FOUSTKA: (*To* VILMA) You'd like that, wouldn't you?

VILMA: (*Softly*) Don't start ...

FOUSTKA: (*Softly*) Who's starting? Me?

DIRECTOR: Quiet, please. I'll enquire upstairs whether she might not be able to take a job as a cleaner with one of the housing administrations.

LORENCOVÁ: That would be a sensible and humane solution...

DIRECTOR: (*To* FOUSTKA) Do you wish to make use of your right to respond to the accusation that has been made against you?

(FOUSTKA *gets up slowly and leans against the desk as if it were a lectern.*)

FOUSTKA: Director, Deputy Director, colleagues. I am confident that my case will be dealt with fairly and objectively, and I assume therefore that when the time comes I shall be given the opportunity to give a more detailed explanation and that some of the circumstances I shall be able to elucidate will lead to my complete vindication. For the time being, however, I shall confine myself to expressing the hope that the investigation will, in keeping with our scientific approach to reality and our scientific morality, be unprejudiced and have the one and only aim of uncovering the truth. Not only in my interest and in the interest of science, which it is the task of our Institute to protect and cultivate, but also in the interests of you all: otherwise my case could easily become merely the first link in a long chain of injustice with consequences I dare not even contemplate. Thank you for your attention.

(FOUSTKA *sits down. An embarrassed pause: they are all uneasy, though each for a different reason.*)

DIRECTOR: We are living in modern times and no one here has the slightest intention of staging a witch-hunt. That would only be to revive the old ignorance and fanaticism, against which we are fighting. Let the manner in which Dr Foustka's case is handled become a model of a truly scientific approach to facts, which will provide inspiration for us all. Truth must prevail, whoever suffers in the process.

(*A short pause.*)

Who has volunteered to tidy up the garden?

KOTRLÝ: I did, Director.

(*The* DIRECTOR *goes to* KOTRLÝ, *who rises. The* DIRECTOR *puts his hand on* KOTRLÝ's *shoulder and looks him gravely in the face. Then, in a voice charged with emotion, he says:*)

DIRECTOR: I am delighted that you have taken on this task, Vilém. I shall come and give you a hand.

(MAGGIE *enters, left, dressed in ordinary clothes and carrying a small suitcase. She has been crying, and crosses the room as if in a trance, leaving by the rear door. As she closes it, the chandelier falls down. It hits no one but smashes into little pieces on the floor. The curtain falls.*)

(*Intermission*)

SCENE SIX

FOUSTKA's *flat. Only* FISTULA *is on stage as the curtain rises. He is sitting behind the desk, examining the papers lying on it. He is wearing slippers, the paper bag containing his shoes is on top of the desk among all the papers.* FOUSTKA, *still wearing his evening clothes, enters. He is startled to find* FISTULA *sitting there.*

FOUSTKA: (*Cries out*) What the ... what're you doing here?

FISTULA: Waiting for you.

FOUSTKA: How did you get in?

FISTULA: No, not down the chimney, if that's what you're worried about. I came in through the door, which Mrs Houbová kindly opened for me before she went off to do her shopping. You see, I explained to her that you urgently wanted to speak to me and that, given my gammy leg, I could hardly be expected to wait outside on the pavement.

FOUSTKA: You mean you lied – as usual ...

FISTULA: Don't you believe I'm an invalid?

FOUSTKA: You lied when you pretended that I was anxious to see you. The truth is, on the contrary, that after everything that's happened, I was hoping never to clap eyes on you again.

FISTULA: On the contrary, what has happened makes our meetings that much more desirable.

FOUSTKA: Be all that as it may – how dare you rummage among my papers?

FISTULA: Well, I had to find something to do while I waited . . .

FOUSTKA: And what about those shoes?

FISTULA: Oh, come now, don't be such an old fusspot . . .

(FISTULA *gives one of his asinine grins, then picks up the paper bag, goes over to the couch and sits down, depositing the bag next to him.*)

Why don't you sit down?

(FOUSTKA, *still angry, crosses to the desk, sits down and looks at* FISTULA.)

Well, what do you say – pretty successful so far, wouldn't you agree?

FOUSTKA: Successful? What might you be referring to?

FISTULA: I'd never have expected you to manage it so quickly and so easily. You're a good learner, I must say.

FOUSTKA: I haven't the slightest idea what you're talking about.

FISTULA: Oh yes, you have. Did we not agree first of all to carry out a little innocent experiment? And it succeeded beyond all expectation, don't you think?

FOUSTKA: If you mean that that wretched child developed a crush on me, let me just tell you two things: first and foremost, that was no work of magic, much less your doing.

All that happened was that I had . . .

FISTULA: Quite by chance . . .

FOUSTKA: Quite by chance, an opportunity to talk to her properly for the first time, and that, as it happens . . .

FISTULA: By chance . . .

FOUSTKA: . . . I was on form that night, so that she found what I had to say interesting. Well, as such girls do, her interest soon switched . . .

FISTULA: By chance . . .

FOUSTKA: . . . from the topic of conversation to the speaker. I can't see anything out of the ordinary in that. And, secondly: seeing what consequences this event had for the girl, I bitterly regret that it ever happened, even though I had no idea – how could I? – that our innocent talk would *have* such consequences . . .

(FISTULA *laughs uproariously, banging his thighs with his hands.*)

Would you mind telling me what's so funny?

FISTULA: (*Grows serious*) My dear Doctor! We all know that you don't believe in such unscientific things as mere chance and the workings of coincidence. You have obviously not asked yourself how it was that you, who up till then were just about capable of requesting her to make you a cup of coffee, were suddenly waxing so eloquently in front of the girl, courageously spouting ideas which you well knew could put your career at the Institute in jeopardy. Does it not seem odd to you that this should have happened just when we had hatched our little scheme? And does it not surprise you that your ideas alone – as if someone had waved a magic wand – overcame all the girl's inhibitions, kindling a love that nothing can destroy?

FOUSTKA: Oh, we all have our moments when we somehow manage to transcend ourselves . . .

FISTULA: Yes, that's just it! That is what I'm talking about!

FOUSTKA: I don't understand . . .

FISTULA: You surely didn't think that the spirit of love, Jeviel, would turn up and arrange everything for you like some mundane matchmaker? How else do you think he could fix it except through you yourself? It's quite simple, really – he, so to speak, took over your body. Or rather, he aroused and liberated something in you that's always been there but had lain dormant until then.

FOUSTKA: You don't say!

FISTULA: The human mind, after all, is not an inert mass – you must know that better than I do, being a scientist. If the seed is to sprout, someone has first to sow it . . .

FOUSTKA: If – I say *if* – you and your . . . whatever-his-name-is . . .

FISTULA: Jeviel . . .

FOUSTKA: If you and your Jeviel *are* in any way responsible for sowing that seed, then I curse the two of you from the bottom of my heart. You're a devil and I don't want to have anything more to do with you.

FISTULA: Why are you being so dense? If the devil exists, then he is within all of us . . .

FOUSTKA: In that case you must be his favourite abode.

FISTULA: You overestimate me, my dear sir, in just the same way as a moment ago you overestimated yourself. I am no more than a catalyst, helping my fellow men to bring out something that exists in them without my intervention. It is just that with my assistance they then find in themselves the courage to lead a more exciting life, to enjoy life to the full and to be more truly themselves. We only live once, so why should we spend those few decades that are allotted to us stifling under the gag of life-denying scruples? You know why you called me a devil? To rid yourself of responsibility – and to ease your conscience by, as the scientists say, 'transferring' or 'projecting' it on to me. I do hope that you will succeed in outwitting your scruples in this way. But you must understand that I – an insignificant invalid – could not budge you by so much as an inch if you did not *want* to be budged, if indeed you had not dreamed about being budged long ago. Our little experiment was merely designed to bring these trivialities home to you.

FOUSTKA: In that case what was all that about its being so innocent? A barefaced lie!

FISTULA: Wrong again! You are once more only trying to lie to yourself. You could easily have told the girl how infallible was the scientific view of the world, you could have expounded on the world-shattering importance of the work your Institute is doing, and she would have been quite safe. And even having chosen the other course, you still didn't have to abandon her so selfishly when it came to the crunch. But that's not the point. I really have to compliment you on one thing – that, for a beginner, you acquitted yourself really well. Your disguise in the saintly habit of an impassioned seeker after (*He points a finger at the ceiling*.) as the true source of the meaning of the universe and of all moral imperatives – that was truly magnificent! I take my hat off to you.

FOUSTKA: (*Angrily*) What disguise? I was saying exactly what I believed to be true.

FISTULA: My dear friend . . .

FOUSTKA: I am no friend of yours!

FISTULA: My dear sir, truth is not merely what we are thinking, but also why, to whom and under what circumstances we say it.

(FOUSTKA *gazes fixedly at* FISTULA *for a few moments, then sadly nods, strides up and down the room a few times, and sits down again. After a short pause he says in a quiet voice:*)

FOUSTKA: I don't know how they managed it, but somehow they've found out that I have had contact with you, and as a result it is highly likely that I'll be fired, made an example of, publicly disgraced, and no doubt completely destroyed. The reason why all this is about to happen to me is – at least where I'm concerned – immaterial. I see the true meaning of my downfall in something else. It will be a just punishment for my unforgivable irresponsibility, for my having succumbed to temptation, under the influence of a poisonous, unsubstantiated, evil jealousy which my over-weening pride caused to grow within me. Thus I tried to kill two birds with one stone, to gain the affections of one and to hurt another. Yes, I was blinded by some devilish impulse in my heart, and I must therefore be grateful to you for helping me realize this – whatever your motives or methods. By awakening both the temptation and the jealousy, you enabled me to see myself from the darker side. Not only that: your explanation has thrown light on the true source of my error, which as you rightly say has to be sought inside me and nowhere else. I therefore do not regret our meeting – if that's the word for the way you insinuated yourself into my life. I have learned an important lesson, and your dark intentions have served to illuminate my own behaviour. I am telling you all this because – I sincerely hope and believe – this is the last time

I shall see you. And that you will leave now, this very
minute.

(*A long pause.* FISTULA *slowly extracts his shoes from the
paper bag, looks at them thoughtfully, smells them, then at last
puts them down on the floor in front of him and turns, smiling,
to* FOUSTKA.)

FISTULA: We are engineers of our own fate. I was going to say
something, but now I'm not sure that it wouldn't be better
to wait until you are – if I may so put it – a little more
receptive . . .

FOUSTKA: No, go on, what did you want to say?

FISTULA: I am as well acquainted with the thought processes
you have just been kind enough to demonstrate for me as I
am with these old shoes of mine. We hermetics call it the
Smíchovský Compensation Syndrome.

FOUSTKA: And what's that when it's at home?

FISTULA: Whenever a beginner successfully breaks the carapace
of his or her earlier inhibitions, thus giving free passage to
all one's latent possibilities, there follows the inevitable
'hangover', accompanied by a bout of what I can only call
masochistic self-accusation and self-chastisement.
Psychologically speaking, this is a perfectly natural
reaction. In his desire to, so to speak, belatedly mollify his
scruples, principles, whatever, the person concerned re-
interprets the action by means of which he betrayed them
so that it becomes a kind of purifying act, a lesson he has
had to learn in order to become a better human being. In
short, he turns it into a sort of little dance-floor on which to
perform the ritual celebration of his principles. Usually it
doesn't take long before he sobers up and comes to realize
something that we of course are well aware of but cannot
explain to him: I mean the grotesque discrepancy between
the worthlessness of the scruples in whose name he
demanded the direst punishment for himself, and the
fundamental value of the experience which he was trying
thus to expiate . . .

(FOUSTKA *jumps up and bangs the desk in fury.*)

FOUSTKA: All right – that's it! If you think for a minute that by your speechifying you're going to inveigle me into some dubious adventure, you're bloody well mistaken!

FISTULA: No, my dear sir, it is you who are mistaken if you fondly believe that you're *not* inveigled already . . .

FOUSTKA: (*Shouts*) Get out!

FISTULA: May I just point out that when you return to reality and, who knows, feel like consulting me, I may not be there to be consulted. However, that is your funeral . . .

FOUSTKA: Just piss off, would you. If it's all right with you, I'd like to be left alone with my Smíchovský Compensation Syndrome.

(FISTULA *slowly picks up his shoes, shaking his head as he does so. Then he throws the shoes on the floor, jumps to his feet and starts to pound his forehead with his hand.*)

FISTULA: I don't believe this! Driven by her unreasoning jealousy because he had the audacity to spend a few minutes in a philosophical discussion with another woman, his mistress shops him to his superiors and tells them he has had contacts with a magician . . .

FOUSTKA: What are you suggesting?

FISTULA: And he would be willing to let them deprive him of his job, his scientific career, perhaps his entire property! Without so much as lifting a finger in his own defence. Well, I've seen a lot in my time but this is something else! Even old Smíchovský himself would have a fit if he heard this!

FOUSTKA: I simply do not believe that Vilma could do something like that. After all the sunny moments of pure happiness we've known together!

FISTULA: That just goes to show how little you know women. It may well be the memory of those sunny moments that provided the motive force for her action.

(FISTULA *calms down, resumes his seat, and slowly removes his slippers. He smells them and then carefully replaces them in the paper bag, then puts on his shoes. A long pause.*)

FOUSTKA: (*Softly*) Well, what would you suggest I do?

FISTULA: Oh, forget it . . .

FOUSTKA: Surely you can tell me?

FISTULA: You should have realized by now that I don't go around dispensing advice or fixing things. At most I'll occasionally provide someone with a stimulus . . .
(*Having put his shoes on,* FISTULA *picks up the paper bag and makes for the door.*)

FOUSTKA: (*Shouts*) Don't talk in riddles, damn you!
(FISTULA *stops, stands stock still for a few moments, then turns round to face* FOUSTKA.)

FISTULA: All you have to do is to summon up, in a good cause, at least a small fraction of the cunning which your dear Director makes use of, in pursuance of wicked causes, from morning till night.
(FISTULA *starts to grin;* FOUSTKA *stares at him in some consternation; the curtain falls.*)

SCENE SEVEN

The same room in the Institute in which Scenes One and Five took place. A naked bulb, suspended by a wire, hangs in place of the chandelier. As the curtain goes up, LORENCOVÁ, KOTRLÝ *and* NEUWIRTH *are on stage.* LORENCOVÁ, *wearing a white coat, is sitting behind the desk, powdering her face, her powder compact propped against the typewriter.* KOTRLÝ, *also in a white coat, is stretched out on the bench, reading a newspaper.* NEUWIRTH, *in ordinary clothes, is standing by the bookcase, his back to the others, examining one of the books. A short pause.*

LORENCOVÁ: Who's now going to make us coffee?

KOTRLÝ: (*Without looking up*) Why don't you go and make it?

LORENCOVÁ: Why don't *you*?
(FOUSTKA *enters quickly by the rear door. He is wearing a black sweater and black trousers, carries a briefcase, is slightly out of breath.*)

FOUSTKA: Hi . . .

NEUWIRTH: (*Without turning round*) Hi.
(*The others do not acknowledge* FOUSTKA's *arrival, each carrying on with what he or she was doing.* FOUSTKA *stands*

*his briefcase on top of the desk and hurriedly extracts some
papers from it.)*

FOUSTKA: Have they been yet?

NEUWIRTH: *(Without turning round)* Not yet.

(When FOUSTKA *realizes that* LORENCOVÁ *will not vacate
the desk for him, he crosses to the bench and sits down next to*
KOTRLÝ. *A pause.)*

LORENCOVÁ: Poor Maggie . . .

*(*FOUSTKA *looks up, attentively.)*

KOTRLÝ: *(Without looking up)* What about her?

LORENCOVÁ: Why, she tried to cut her wrists . . .

*(*FOUSTKA *gets to his feet, agitated.)*

KOTRLÝ: *(Without looking up)* So it is true . . .

NEUWIRTH: *(Without turning round)* They say she's in the
psycho ward . . .

LORENCOVÁ: The poor thing . . .

*(*FOUSTKA *sits down again. The* DEPUTY *enters, right, in
ordinary clothes, holding hands with* PETRUŠKA, *who is
wearing a white coat.* LORENCOVÁ *puts her mirror and
compact in her coat pocket;* KOTRLÝ *folds his newspaper;*
NEUWIRTH *puts back the book and turns round;*
LORENCOVÁ, KOTRLÝ *and* FOUSTKA *get up.)*

KOTRLÝ: Good morning, sir.

DEPUTY: Good morning, friends. Sit down, sit down, please . . .

*(*LORENCOVÁ, KOTRLÝ *and* FOUSTKA *resume their seats. A
short pause.)*

I don't see Vilma here.

FOUSTKA: She's had to go to the dentist.

(A short pause.)

DEPUTY: As you all know, we have a difficult task before us
today. No one here – as the Director so aptly put it – has
any intention of carrying out a witch-hunt. Truth must
prevail, whoever suffers in the process. But all the more
reason for us to remember that to seek the truth means to
seek the *whole* and unembellished truth. The truth, my
friends, is not just that which is shown to be true, but also
that which it serves or for which it may be misused. As
scientists we are only too acutely aware that by taking a fact

out of its context we can completely alter its meaning, indeed we can stand it on its head and thus turn truth into a lie and vice versa. In short, we must not lose sight of the living background of the actions we'll be judging and of the conclusions we come to. I hope I need not say any more – we're not little children, after all. Or are we?

KOTRLÝ: No, we're not.

DEPUTY: There you are, then! Who's feeding the pigeons today?

NEUWIRTH: I am . . .

DEPUTY: Splendid.

(*The* DIRECTOR *enters, right, in a white coat.* LORENCOVÁ, KOTRLÝ *and* FOUSTKA *rise quickly.*)

KOTRLÝ: Hi.

DIRECTOR: Hullo there, friends. Do sit down, please . . .

(LORENCOVÁ, KOTRLÝ *and* FOUSTKA *sit down. A short pause.*)

Where is Vilma?

DEPUTY: I asked the same question. I understand she's had to go to the dentist.

(*The* DIRECTOR *goes up to* KOTRLÝ *and holds out his hand to him.* KOTRLÝ *gets up.*)

DIRECTOR: (*To* KOTRLÝ) Did you sleep well?

KOTRLÝ: Yes, very well, thank you.

(*The* DIRECTOR *squeezes* KOTRLÝ'*s elbow in a friendly fashion and turns to the others.* KOTRLÝ *sits down again.*)

DIRECTOR: As you all know, we have a difficult task before us today.

DEPUTY: That's just what I told our colleagues just now, Director.

DIRECTOR: We all know what is at stake, so you'll forgive me if I dispense with the preliminaries . . .

(VILMA *comes running in through the rear door. She seems out of breath, is carrying a large cardboard box.*)

VILMA: Sorry to be late, Director – I had an appointment with my dentist this morning, and just imagine . . .

DIRECTOR: Yes, I've heard. Sit down.

(VILMA *sits on the couch, puts the box down by her feet, and tries to communicate with* FOUSTKA *in mime, then she indicates to him that she is keeping her fingers crossed.* LORENCOVÁ *leans over to her.*)

LORENCOVÁ: (*Softly*) What did you get?

VILMA: (*Softly*) Just my micro-oven back from the repair shop.

LORENCOVÁ: (*Softly*) Oh, I thought you'd bought a new hat.

VILMA: (*Softly.*) No ...

DIRECTOR: Where was I?

KOTRLÝ: You were saying that we'll forgive you if you dispense with the preliminaries ...

DIRECTOR: Oh yes. Let us dispense with the preliminaries and come straight to the point. Dr Foustka, would you please ... (*The* DIRECTOR *motions to* FOUSTKA *that he is to come forward;* FOUSTKA *gets up, crosses to centre stage and stands on the spot indicated by the* DIRECTOR.)
Good. Shall we begin?

FOUSTKA: By all means.

DIRECTOR: Well then, Dr Foustka, can you tell us whether it is true that for some time now ...
(*The* SECRETARY *enters, right. He goes to the* DIRECTOR, *and whispers at length in his ear, the* DIRECTOR *nodding all the time and looking serious. The* SECRETARY *stops whispering, the* DIRECTOR *nods for the last time, the* SECRETARY *leaves, right.*)
Now, where was I?

KOTRLÝ: You were asking him if it is true that for some time ...

DIRECTOR: Ah yes. Well then, Dr Foustka, can you tell us whether it is true that for some time now you have been engaged in the study of what is known as hermetic literature?

FOUSTKA: Yes, that's quite true.

DEPUTY: How long, would you say?

FOUSTKA: Oh, I can't say exactly ...

DEPUTY: Approximately, then: six months, a year ...?

FOUSTKA: Something like that.

DIRECTOR: How many such books would you say you'd read in that time?

FOUSTKA: Oh, I don't know ... I didn't count them.

DEPUTY: Approximately: Five? Thirty? Fifty?

FOUSTKA: Yes, maybe fifty ...

DIRECTOR: Whom did you lend them to?

FOUSTKA: Lend them? Why, to no one.

DEPUTY: Come, come, Dr Foustka, are you trying to tell us that *nobody* borrowed these sought-after, rare and today practically unobtainable books? Your friends must have seen them, surely.

FOUSTKA: I don't invite friends to my place, and I don't lend books as a matter of principle.

DIRECTOR: All right. Now I must ask you to listen carefully, this is a most important question. I'm going to ask you. What made you take up this study in the first place? Why did you start taking such an interest in these things?

FOUSTKA: I had for some time been disturbed by the increasing interest taken by young people in everything that had to do with the so-called supernatural. This led finally to my deciding to write a study in which I would set out to show how diametrically opposed are the various idealistic and mystical beliefs of the past to our contemporary knowledge of the world. My project of course required ...

DIRECTOR: (*Interrupts* FOUSTKA) That is exactly how we would have expected you to respond to my question. It does nothing, however, to explain the shocking fact that you yourself allegedly practised magic ...

FOUSTKA: Well, hardly. I let it be known that I was practising it but did very little practising in actual fact ...

DIRECTOR: But why would you do that?

FOUSTKA: It was the only way I could gain the confidence of someone as distrustful as are today's magicians.

DIRECTOR: I see. Are you saying you desired to be taken into their confidence? That is most interesting, most interesting. And to what extent, would you say, did you succeed?

FOUSTKA: To the modest extent, for the time being, of attracting the attention of a certain individual who has now visited me twice, as you have no doubt been informed ...

DIRECTOR: Did that individual tell you *why* he visited you ?

FOUSTKA: He said he knew that I was interested in magical practices and that he was willing to initiate me in them.

DIRECTOR: And you accepted?

FOUSTKA: No, not in so many words – on the other hand I didn't explicitly turn him down. We are, so to speak, at the stage of preliminary soundings.

DEPUTY: What is he asking in return?

FOUSTKA: That I should, if need be, confirm that he has put himself at the disposal of science . . .

DEPUTY: Did you hear that, Director! Very clever, I must say . . .

DIRECTOR: I think the time has come to pose our crucial question: how do you explain that, on the one hand, you claim to have a scientific view of the world and therefore know that anyone pretending to be a magician is nothing but a charlatan, and yet, on the other, here you are trying to gain the confidence of magicians and when one of them actually seeks you out, you not only don't scorn him and throw him out, you actually intend to collaborate with him, indeed perhaps even shield him? Such obscure contacts and activities can hardly be brushed off by reference to critical scientific research.

FOUSTKA: This may seem naïve to you, but I simply felt, right from the outset, that I must not confine my efforts to help those who are being led astray by these charlatans – and my intention to do something effective about it – to mere theorizing and propaganda. I was and remain convinced that it would be dishonest of me if I were permanently to avoid tackling living reality just so as to keep a clear conscience and to try and deceive myself with illusions of the far-reaching effects of my theoretical struggle. I simply felt that having taken the first step, it was up to me to continue the journey, and that it was my duty as a citizen to place my theoretical knowledge at the disposal of the campaign to unmask and bring to book the perpetrators of these activities. Now at the Institute we are all the time professing to be fighting against pseudo-science, mysticism and superstition – and yet we would be hard put to it to

point a finger at even one of those who spread these poisons. And not just us – it is nothing short of amazing how little is known about these matters, how unsuccessful all the attempts to infiltrate these murky waters. No wonder then that the disease is spreading so rapidly. That is why I decided to gain the confidence of these people, penetrate their circle and collect damning evidence at the very source. I can hardly do this without pretending to share at least some of their beliefs in spirits, initiations, evocations, magic happenings, incubi and succubi, and all the rest of that nonsense. I may even have to take an oath of silence if I wish to string them along. In short, I've decided to be an inconspicuous, lone soldier in this – how shall I put it? – in this secret war, having come to the conclusion that my expertise makes me particularly suitable for this task . . .
(*A long pause. All his listeners are taken aback, looking at one another in puzzlement, then they all fix their eyes on the* DIRECTOR.)

DIRECTOR: You mean to say that you . . . that . . . well, I . . .
(*A pause.*)
Well, I cannot deny that it would be a feather in our cap if the Institute could bring off some such successful coup. Dr Foustka is doubtless right when he says that no propaganda brochures ever won a war . . .

DEPUTY: (*To* FOUSTKA) Am I to understand then that you would be willing to provide us with a record of any and every meeting you might have, either with this individual of yours or with anyone else?

FOUSTKA: But of course – that's why I've got into this in the first place . . .

DEPUTY: Well, I cannot deny that that would be a feather in our cap, as the Director has already pointed out. Tell me one thing, though – why is it that this . . . this commendable initiative of yours has only come to our notice now, when certain – it would seem unsubstantiated – accusations have been levelled against you? Why did you not inform us about your intentions and about the first steps you took right from the beginning?

FOUSTKA: Yes, I can see now that that was a mistake. I approached the whole business as a scientist about to undertake a new line of research. As you know, we scientists tend to work on our own, we are not in the habit of reporting every step, and I thought it would be time enough to report progress when I had actually achieved something worthy of reporting. It just did not occur to me that a tit-bit of information from some uninformed source could possibly shake the confidence I had hitherto enjoyed at the Institute.

DIRECTOR: That is hardly surprising, wouldn't you say? However noble your idea, what you have done is so out of the ordinary and, if I may say so, so unexpected in your particular case that we cannot be blamed if at first we misunderstood your motives.

DEPUTY: That is hardly surprising, wouldn't you say?

DIRECTOR: But never mind – let us not waste any more time, we all have work to do. You have convinced me that it *was* just a misunderstanding, and all that remains to be said is that I am glad that it has now been satisfactorily cleared up. Needless to say, I appreciate what you are trying to do and I shall see to it that your remarkable initiative is suitably rewarded – particularly once you get into the habit of keeping a record of your researches and regularly passing it on to us. Any questions, anyone?

(*An embarrassed pause.*)

Nothing? In that case, let me spring my little surprise: tomorrow's social in the Institute garden will be in fancy dress!

LORENCOVÁ: Fabulous!

KOTRLÝ: What a marvellous idea!

DEPUTY: Isn't it? I quite agree . . .

LORENCOVÁ: What theme will it have?

DIRECTOR: Obviously – Witches' Sabbath!

(*An excited murmur.*)

A congregation of devils, witches, magicians and sorcerers. We'll do it in style. Originally I had thought of it simply as an attempt to enliven our tradition of Institute socials by the addition of a parodic element. It seemed to me that if, in the evening, we were to laugh at that which, during the day, we have to combat with a cool head and straight face, we could enhance our own attitude to our work – in keeping with the latest findings of costume therapy. By momentarily ridiculing the problem, we would be emphasizing its lasting gravity; by making light of it, drawing attention to its weightiness; by standing aside from it, drawing closer to it. Now, however, I see that, thanks to the coincidence of Dr Foustka's revelations, there is also another way of looking at it: as a light-hearted tribute to his admirable efforts, which may well necessitate not only disguise in the figurative sense of the world, but also disguise in the literal sense, if he, for instance, has to infiltrate a black mass.

(*Polite laughter.*)

But never mind – let us not waste any more time, we all have work to do. Perhaps we can consider this to be a bit of light relief after our serious session, which has been so satisfactorily concluded. Whose turn is it to feed the pigeons?

NEUWIRTH: Mine . . .

DIRECTOR: Splendid. (*To* KOTRLÝ) Now, don't forget, Vilém! (*Curtain falls.*)

SCENE EIGHT

VILMA's *flat. As the curtain rises,* FOUSTKA *is sitting in his underpants on the edge of the bed,* VILMA, *wearing a lace negligée, is combing her hair by the dressing-table – the same situation as at the beginning of Scene Four.*

FOUSTKA: Once you let him in I'm sure he'd expect a little more than a kiss on the cheek! At the very least he'd want to dance with you.

VILMA: Henry, please leave it alone. After all, I don't give *you* the third degree – even though I have more reason than you.

(*A short pause, then* FOUSTKA *gets up and starts pacing up and down the room, lost in thought.* VILMA *stops combing her hair and follows him with her eyes.*)
What is it?

FOUSTKA: What's what?

VILMA: You started off so nicely . . .

FOUSTKA: Somehow I don't feel like it today . . .

VILMA: Does it excite you too much?

FOUSTKA: No, it's not that.

VILMA: So what's wrong?

FOUSTKA: As if you didn't know . . .

VILMA: But I don't!

FOUSTKA: You don't, do you? Who shopped me, who told the Director that the magician had come to see me?
(VILMA *freezes, then throws her comb down, jumps up and looks at* FOUSTKA, *horrified.*)

VILMA: For heaven's sake, Henry, you don't really think . . .

FOUSTKA: No one else at the Institute knew about it.

VILMA: Are you crazy? Why should I do a thing like that? Quite apart from insulting me by believing for a moment that I would be capable of denouncing anybody to that idiot, how can you think that I would inform on *you*? I would as soon go and inform on myself! Don't you know how much I want you to be happy and how much I worry about you? What possible reason would I suddenly have to try and destroy you? And with you, to destroy myself – our relationship – our life together – our make-believe jealousy – our love, which you have recently confirmed so deliciously by exhibiting *real* jealousy – our memories of all the sunny moments of pure happiness we have known together . . . Why, it would be sheer madness!

FOUSTKA: It may well be the memory of those sunny moments that provided the motive force for your action. What do I know about women? Perhaps you wanted to take revenge on me because of Maggie – or perhaps you were scared of that invalid and thought that in this way you could extricate me from what you considered to be his clutches . . .
(VILMA *runs to the bed, throws herself face down on the*

pillow, and starts crying. FOUSTKA *stands there helplessly, looking at* VILMA, *then he sits down gingerly on the bed and strokes her hair.*)

Come on now, Vilma...

(*A pause.* VILMA *goes on sobbing.*)

I didn't mean it...

(*A pause.* VILMA *goes on sobbing.*)

It was just a joke...

(*A pause.* VILMA *goes on sobbing.*)

I thought I'd add a new twist to our game...

(*A pause.* VILMA *sits up abruptly, wiping her eyes with her handkerchief and sniffling. When she has recovered her composure, she says coolly:*)

VILMA: Go away!

(FOUSTKA *attempts to stroke her, but* VILMA *pushes him away and shouts.*)

Don't touch me! Go away!

FOUSTKA: Really, Vilma. Why're you making such a fuss? You've often asked me to say far worse things to you...

VILMA: That was different. Do you realize what you've done? You've accused me in so many words of spying on you! Kindly get dressed and go away – and don't ever try to patch up what you've just so brutally destroyed.

FOUSTKA: Are you serious?

VILMA: Let's end it here and now. It would have come to that sooner or later...

FOUSTKA: You mean on account of that dancer?

VILMA: No, not that...

FOUSTKA: Why then?

VILMA: I've lost my respect for you.

FOUSTKA: Well, that's a new one on me.

VILMA: It's only just happened, that's why. Today, if you must know, at the Institute – it struck me then, when I saw how shamelessly you got yourself out of a hole. In front of everybody, to tell the Director that you'd act as a stool-pigeon for him. And now, to cap it all, you come and accuse *me* of acting like one! Can't you see how absurd it all is? What's got into you? Is this really you I'm talking to?

Or has some devil truly possessed you? That wretched
fellow has addled your brain, I expect. God knows what
he's done to you, what kind of magic he's trying out on
you . . .

(FOUSTKA *gets up and starts pacing up and down the room.*)

FOUSTKA: All right, I'll tell you what he has done. No magic
tricks: he is merely helping me to know myself better and
to counter the bad things lying dormant inside me. Listen,
my acting as a stool-pigeon, as you put it, not only served
to save me but also to help him – the only way I could. If
they know that I'm in control, they'll leave him alone.
Anyway, how could I keep my suspicion that you betrayed
me to myself? What kind of a relationship would that be?
You may have said it inadvertently, perhaps to someone
you trusted, or perhaps it was overheard by someone whose
presence you were unaware of.

VILMA: I didn't say anything to anybody, inadvertently or
otherwise – and it's not your expressing your suspicion that
I object to – even though you did it so brutally and are
now, belatedly, trying to wriggle out of it – what I mind is
that you could even *think* such a thing. If you can do that,
even for a minute, then I don't see how we can stay
together.

(*A pause.* FOUSTKA *sinks into the armchair and gazes
dispiritedly in front of him.*)

FOUSTKA: What an idiot I was to say anything. But then, I
always manage to mess things up, don't I? What am I going
to do without you? How can I go on living if I'm to lose
you?

VILMA: Now you're going to feel sorry for yourself, are you?

FOUSTKA: Do you remember what we said to each other that
day by the river under the elms?

VILMA: It'll do you no good to remind me. You've hurt me too
much for you to talk your way out of it by dredging up our
memories. And anyway, I asked you to go . . .

FOUSTKA: I know what it is – you're expecting the dancer,
aren't you?

VILMA: I'm not expecting anybody – I just want to be alone.

(*A short pause.* FOUSTKA *suddenly jumps up, runs across to* VILMA, *pushes her down on the bed and roughly seizes her by the throat.*)

FOUSTKA: (*In a menacing voice*) You're lying, you bitch!

VILMA: (*Cries out*) Help!

(FOUSTKA *is throttling* VILMA. *The door bell rings.* FOUSTKA *lets go of* VILMA, *jumps away from the bed, remains standing there for a few moments, then slowly goes to the armchair and sits down heavily.* VILMA *gets up, hurriedly arranges her hair and her clothing, and goes to the door. She opens it to find the* DANCER *outside, a bunch of violets held behind his back.*)

DANCER: Sorry to show up so late. I only wanted to give you ...

(*The* DANCER *hands the flowers to* VILMA.)

VILMA: Thanks. Do come in, won't you.

(*The* DANCER, *surprised, looks first at* VILMA, *then at* FOUSTKA, *who is sitting slumped in the armchair, staring vacantly in front of him.*)

He's not well ... I'd be glad if you could stay. I'm afraid that ...

DANCER: Is it his heart?

VILMA: Probably.

DANCER: Why don't we dance a little? Maybe it will cheer him up ...

(*Curtain falls.*)

SCENE NINE

FOUSTKA's *flat.* FOUSTKA *is alone, in a dressing-gown, pacing up and down the room. There is a knock on the door.* FOUSTKA *stops pacing, hesitates for a moment, then calls out.*

FOUSTKA: (*Calls out*) Who is it?

HOUBOVÁ: (*Off stage*) It's only me, Doctor.

FOUSTKA: (*Calling*) Come in, Mrs Houbová.

(HOUBOVÁ *enters.*)

HOUBOVÁ: You have a visitor ...

FOUSTKA: Have I? Who is it?

HOUBOVÁ: It's him again. You know, the one who . . .

FOUSTKA: I know – smells.

HOUBOVÁ: That's him.

FOUSTKA: Tell him to come in.

(*A short pause.* HOUBOVÁ *stands still, embarrassed.*)

Well, what is it?

HOUBOVÁ: I don't know how . . .

FOUSTKA: What is the matter?

HOUBOVÁ: Look 'ere, Doctor, I'm just an ignorant woman . . .
I know it's not my place to give you advice . . .

FOUSTKA: No, go on, what is it you want to tell me?

HOUBOVÁ: I know it's none of my business, but if I were you, I
wouldn't trust him. I can't explain . . . and I don't know
why he comes here in the first place, but he . . . well, he
gives me the creeps . . .

FOUSTKA: You let him in readily enough last time.

HOUBOVÁ: 'Cause I was afraid of him, that's why.

FOUSTKA: Well, I know he looks somewhat odd, but he is quite
harmless, you know. Or, more precisely, he's too
insignificant to be in a position to do too much damage.

HOUBOVÁ: I don't know why you have any truck with such as
'im. A gentleman like you.

FOUSTKA: Oh, come, Mrs Houbová, I'm over eighteen and
perfectly capable of looking after myself.

HOUBOVÁ: I'm afraid for your sake. And is it surprising – why,
I remember you as a little three-year-old, me not having
children of my own . . .

FOUSTKA: Yes, yes, I know. Thank you for your concern – you
must not think I don't appreciate it, but in this case you
really need have no fear. Just let him in and stop worrying.

(HOUBOVÁ *leaves the room, leaving the door ajar.*)

HOUBOVÁ: (*Off stage*) You're to go in . . .

(FISTULA *enters, holding his paper bag in his hand.*
HOUBOVÁ *stands in the doorway, following him with her eyes,
then she shakes her head and closes the door.* FISTULA *grins
vacuously and makes straight for the couch, sits down, takes his
shoes off, removes his slippers from the bag and puts them on,*

replacing them in the bag with his shoes, then lays the bag on the floor at his feet. He looks up at FOUSTKA *and grins.*)

FISTULA: Well . . .?

FOUSTKA: Well, what?

FISTULA: I'm waiting for you to start your usual litany . . .

FOUSTKA: What're you talking about?

FISTULA: Telling me to get out and so on . . .

(FOUSTKA *paces up and down the room, then sits down at his desk.*)

FOUSTKA: I see. Now look, I'd just like to say a couple of things. Firstly, I've realized that there's no way I can be rid of you, so it's a waste of time and effort to try. Secondly, without in any way overestimating your so-called stimulating influence, I have come to the conclusion that the time spent with you does not have to be entirely wasted. If I have to serve you for your purposes, there is no reason why you should not reciprocate by serving mine in return. Did you not at the outset offer to initiate me into your mysteries if I agree to shield you? Well, I accept your offer.

FISTULA: Yes, I knew you would in the end, which explains why I was so persistent. How nice to see my persistence rewarded at last. But let me not overdo the modesty – I don't ascribe your decision to my persistence alone, but also to the undoubted success of our collaboration . . .

FOUSTKA: What success do you have in mind?

FISTULA: Well, not only have you managed to keep your job at the Institute, you have actually strengthened your position there. I was delighted to notice that you in this case even managed to avoid Smíchovský's Compensation Syndrome – now that is what I call progress . . .

FOUSTKA: If by that you mean that I've jettisoned all my moral principles and left myself open to whatever you may choose to waken in me, then you are very much mistaken. I have not changed, I have only gained a little more self-control, which enables me to know exactly how far I can go without the risk of doing anything I'd later have reason to regret. (FISTULA *grows somewhat agitated, looks around the room.*) What's the matter with you?

FISTULA: It's nothing . . .

FOUSTKA: You look scared. I've never seen that before. Surprising that it should happen now, just when I have promised to shield you.

(FISTULA *takes off his slippers and sighing, rubs the soles of his feet with both hands*.)

Are you in pain?

FISTULA: It's nothing . . . it'll pass . . .

(*After a while* FISTULA *puts his slippers on again. Suddenly he bursts out laughing*.)

FOUSTKA: What's so funny?

FISTULA: May I be absolutely frank?

FOUSTKA: Be my guest.

FISTULA: You are!

FOUSTKA: You're laughing at me, is that it? Of all the bloody cheek!

(FISTULA *grows serious and looks at the floor. After a few moments he glances sharply at* FOUSTKA.)

FISTULA: Look here, Doctor. There's nothing wrong with you saving your skin by dint of a little skulduggery – after all, that's precisely the procedure that Haajah and I . . .

FOUSTKA: Who?

FISTULA: Haajah, the spirit of politics. We prompted you to act as you did. But you shouldn't have forgotten the rules of the game.

FOUSTKA: Rules? What game? What the devil are you talking about?

FISTULA: Does it not occur to you that, like everything else, our collaboration also has its rules? Do away with your scruples as much as you like – you know that I'm all in favour of that. But you really shouldn't try and cheat the one who is guiding you on this exciting, I might perhaps say revolutionary, path you know. Revolution, too, has its rules. Last time you called me a devil. Just imagine for a moment that I really am one. How do you think I'd react to your amateurish attempt to fool me?

FOUSTKA: Fool you? But I wasn't . . .

FISTULA: Look, even if we didn't explicitly promise, surely it should have been obvious that we would not mention our collaboration to anyone, much less write official reports for those in authority who take a negative view of it. I don't think I exaggerate when I say that we had begun – however tentatively – to trust each other. If you failed to grasp that we had this unwritten gentleman's agreement and chose to flout it, then that was your first serious error. You have read enough books on the subject to know that even in my sphere there are limits that cannot be ignored. Surely you must realize that, being able to play with the entire world, we have to put our trust in contacts that simply cannot be trifled with. To lie to a liar is fine, to lie to those who speak the truth is permissible, but to lie to the very powers which furnish us with the ability to lie and ensure that we do so with impunity – that's really unforgivable. As for him (*He points up at the ceiling*), he loads man with a multitude of unrealistic commandments, and so he has no alternative but to forgive, from time to time. Others, on the contrary, liberate man from all these impossible commands, and as a result of course they do not have the need, the opportunity, or ultimately the ability to forgive. Even if they had, they could scarcely forgive someone who goes back on the agreement that opens up all this boundless freedom. Their entire world would collapse, were they to do that. The truth of the matter is, that only by undertaking to be faithful to the authority that gives us this freedom can we hope to be freed. Do you follow my drift?

(FOUSTKA *who, while* FISTULA *was speaking, exhibited increasing signs of nervousness, gets up and starts pacing up and down the room. A long pause.* FISTULA *does not take his eyes off* FOUSTKA, *who suddenly stops behind his desk, leans against it as if it were a lectern, and turns to* FISTULA.)

FOUSTKA: Yes, I understand exactly what you're saying, but I'm afraid you fail to understand *me*.

FISTULA: You don't say.

FOUSTKA: The understanding you are obviously referring to could only be considered as an attempt at treachery on my part by someone who was unaware of the reason why I was able to give it in the first place.

FISTULA: You did it to save your skin . . .

FOUSTKA: Yes, of course, but what would that have been worth had it been paid for by treachery? Do you take me for an idiot? I could give that undertaking only because I had made up my mind from the start not only not to keep it, but at the same time to make the best use of the position I have gained with its help – naturally in close consultation with you, in the spirit of our agreement and for our benefit. In other words, I am now in a position to know exactly what the other side is up to and to flood them with our disinformation; I can cover our tracks and provide them with false ones; and I can use all this to help those of us who are in danger and sink those who endanger us. Don't you see, I can serve our cause like an agent planted in the very midst of the enemy, indeed, at the head of the very department whose job it is to wage war against us. I am surprised and disappointed that you have failed to grasp and appreciate my intentions.

(FOUSTKA sits down. FISTULA jumps to his feet, starts to chortle and hop around the room. Suddenly he stops and, serious again, turns to FOUSTKA.)

FISTULA: Even though you may well have invented this explanation on the spur of the moment – so be it, I accept it. To give you your last chance, you understand. We, too, can occasionally forgive and offer the culprit the opportunity to reform. If a little while ago I told you otherwise, then that was only to scare you and coax you to make this quite unambiguous offer, thus saving you from the very edge of the precipice. As you can see, I really am not the devil – luckily for you: the piece of treachery you have been able to get away with in my case would have cost you dear if I were.

(FOUSTKA is obviously relieved; on a sudden impulse he comes up to FISTULA and embraces him. FISTULA jumps away from him, begins to rub his arms, his teeth chattering.)

Man, your temperature must be a hundred below!

FOUSTKA: (*Laughs*) Not quite . . .
(*Curtain falls.*)

SCENE TEN

We are again in the Institute garden. Everything is the same as in Scene Three, except that the bench is now right and the refreshments table left. When the curtain rises, the music grows softer and changes its character, just as in Scene Three; it again – unless stated otherwise – forms a background to the action. On stage are the two LOVERS *and* FOUSTKA. *The* LOVERS *can be seen dancing at the back, as they will continue to do throughout – the summer-house is thus empty.* FOUSTKA *is sitting on the bench, lost in thought. All three are dressed in accordance with the 'magical theme' of the evening:* FOUSTKA *has come as Faust. Where the text does not provide a more exact description of the costumes or masks, it is to be understood that all the characters appearing in this scene are dressed and made up in the same spirit, and it is left to the producers how this is done. It is to be expected that the costumes and masks will include some of the traditional ones used in the theatre for this type of scene – for instance, the colours black and red will predominate, the characters will be wearing various pendants and amulets, ladies will have frizzy wigs, and there will be a profusion of devils' tails, hooves and chains. The actors, however, behave as if there were no such costumes, their demeanour being just the same as in Scene Three. A long pause. Then* LORENCOVÁ *appears on the right, carrying a broom under her arm. She crosses the stage towards the refreshments table and pours herself a drink. A pause.*
FOUSTKA: Do you know if the Director is here yet?
LORENCOVÁ: No, I don't.
(*A pause.* LORENCOVÁ *finishes her drink, puts down the glass, and goes off, left. A little later we see her dancing, alone with her broom, at the back. A pause. The* DEPUTY *enters, left.*)
DEPUTY: Have you seen Petruška?
FOUSTKA: She's not been here . . .
(*The* DEPUTY *shakes his head, as if in disbelief, and goes off, right. A little later we see him, moving around on the dance-*

floor on his own. FOUSTKA *gets up, crosses to the table, and pours himself a drink. The* DIRECTOR *and* KOTRLÝ *come in from the right, holding hands. Unless stated otherwise, they will remain like that throughout. The* DIRECTOR, *strikingly dressed as a devil, is wearing a pair of horns. The* DIRECTOR *and* KOTRLÝ *pay no attention to* FOUSTKA; *they come to a halt centre stage.* FOUSTKA *watches them.*)

DIRECTOR: (*To* KOTRLÝ) Where are you thinking of putting it?

KOTRLÝ: Seems to me the summer-house would be the best place . . .

DIRECTOR: Yes, I think you're right. For safety reasons, if nothing else . . .

KOTRLÝ: I'll light it in the gardener's shed and then carry it over. It takes a few minutes to get going. I'll put it in the summer-house and a minute or two later – whoosh!

(*The* DIRECTOR *and* KOTRLÝ *start off to the left.*)

FOUSTKA: Oh, Director . . .

(*The* DIRECTOR *and* KOTRLÝ *stop.*)

DIRECTOR: Yes, what is it, Doctor Foustka?

FOUSTKA: Have you got a minute?

DIRECTOR: Sorry, my friend, but not just now . . .

(*The* DIRECTOR *and* KOTRLÝ *go off, left. A little later we see them dancing together at the back. Glass in hand,* FOUSTKA *returns to the bench, lost in thought, and sits down. The music grows noticeably louder, it's a well-known tango.* VILMA *and the* DANCER *come running in, left, and dance together, the* DANCER – *obviously a true professional – leading her in some complicated tango movements.* FOUSTKA *sits there, motionless, looking at them. The music reaches a crescendo,* VILMA *and the* DANCER *end their dance with a final flourish. The music grows softer and changes its character again.* VILMA *and the* DANCER *are out of breath but obviously very happy; they hold hands and smile at each other.*)

FOUSTKA: Having a good time?

VILMA: As you can see . . .

(*The* DEPUTY *having left the dance-floor, enters, left.*)

DEPUTY: Have you seen Petruška?

VILMA: She's not been here . . .

(The DEPUTY *shakes his head, as if in disbelief, and goes off, right. A little later we see him, moving around the dance-floor on his own.* VILMA *seizes the* DANCER *by the hand and leads him off, right. A little later we again see them dancing at the back.* FOUSTKA *gets up, crosses to the refreshments table, and pours himself a drink. The* DIRECTOR *and* KOTRLÝ *come in from the right, having left the dance-floor; they are holding hands. They pay no attention to* FOUSTKA *and come to a halt centre stage.* FOUSTKA *watches them.)*

KOTRLÝ: *(To the* DIRECTOR*)* How do I know the right moment has come?

DIRECTOR: Oh, just pick your own time. Or I'll give you a sign ... I have other things on my mind right now...

KOTRLÝ: What is it?

DIRECTOR: Can you guarantee that nothing will go wrong?

KOTRLÝ: What could go wrong?

DIRECTOR: Well, can't something catch fire, or someone might suffocate...

KOTRLÝ: No, don't worry.

(The DIRECTOR *and* KOTRLÝ *start off to the left.)*

FOUSTKA: Oh, Director ...

(The DIRECTOR *and* KOTRLÝ *stop.)*

DIRECTOR: Yes, what is it, Doctor Foustka?

FOUSTKA: I'm sorry, I know you have a lot of other things on your mind, but this won't take a minute, and...

DIRECTOR: No, really, not just now...

(The SECRETARY *enters, right. He goes to the* DIRECTOR *and whispers at length in his ear, the* DIRECTOR *nodding all the time. While this is going on,* LORENCOVÁ *enters, right, having left the dance-floor. She is still carrying her broom and remains standing, right, by the bench, looking at the* SECRETARY. *After a while the* SECRETARY *stops whispering in the* DIRECTOR'*s ear, the* DIRECTOR *nods for the last time, then goes off, left, with* KOTRLÝ. *A little later we see them dancing together at the back. The* SECRETARY *crosses to the right, in* LORENCOVÁ'*s direction.* LORENCOVÁ *is smiling at him, the* SECRETARY *stops right in front of her and they gaze into each other's eyes, then the* SECRETARY, *without taking his eyes off*

her, takes away her broom, carefully lays it on the ground, and embraces her. She returns his embrace, they stand there gazing tenderly at each other, then they kiss. A few moments later they go off, their arms around each other's waist. A little later we see them dancing together at the back. FOUSTKA *goes back to the bench, glass in hand, and sits down, lost in thought. Suddenly he sits up, as if listening: off stage we hear a girl's voice singing, to the accompaniment of the background music, Ophelia's song from* Hamlet.)

MAGGIE: (*Sings off stage*) And will he not come again?
And will he not come again?
   No, no, he is dead:
   Go to thy death-bed:
He never will come again.
(MAGGIE *appears, left. She is barefoot, has let her hair down and is wearing a wreath of wild flowers, a white nightgown which is stamped at the bottom with a large rubber stamp:* PSYCHIATRY. *She approaches slowly, singing. As she comes towards* FOUSTKA, *he gets up, startled.*)
(*Sings*) He never will come again.
His beard was as white as snow,
All flaxen was his poll:
   He is gone, he is gone,
   And we cast away moan:
God ha' mercy on his soul!
God ha' mercy on his soul!

FOUSTKA: (*Calls out*) Maggie!

MAGGIE: Where is the handsome Prince of Denmark?
(FOUSTKA *retreats in horror, followed by* MAGGIE; *they slowly circle the stage.*)

FOUSTKA: What for God's sake are you doing here? Have you run away?

MAGGIE: Please tell him, if you see him, that it cannot all be happening of its own accord, there has to be a more profound will at work, willing our existence, the world, all nature ...

FOUSTKA: Maggie, don't you recognize me? It's me, Henry ...

MAGGIE: Or does it not strike you as if the cosmos had actually determined to see itself one day through our eyes and to put the questions which we are now putting, with our lips?

FOUSTKA: Go back, Maggie, they will help you get better . . . everything will be all right again . . . you'll see . . .

MAGGIE: (*Sings*) How should I your true love know
　　From another one?
By his cockle hat and staff,
　　And his sandal shoon.

(MAGGIE *goes off, right, her song can still be heard growing fainter, though we can no longer distinguish the words.*
FOUSTKA *agitated, crosses to the table and quickly pours himself a drink, downs it in a single gulp and pours another.*
The DIRECTOR *and* KOTRLÝ *come in, right, having left the dance-floor. They are holding hands and pay no attention to* FOUSTKA.)

DIRECTOR: (*To* KOTRLÝ) At the very least, I'm sure he wanted to dance with you . . .

KOTRLÝ: Please leave it alone! Can't you find something more interesting to talk about?

DIRECTOR: Did he or didn't he?

KOTRLÝ: All right, if you must know, he did. And that's all I'm going to say . . .

(*The* DIRECTOR *and* KOTRLÝ *have slowly crossed the stage and are about to go off, left.*)

FOUSTKA: Oh, Director . . .

(*The* DIRECTOR *and* KOTRLÝ *stop.*)

DIRECTOR: Yes, what is it, Doctor Foustka?

(*At that moment we hear a cry of pain from the bushes behind the bench.*)

NEUWIRTH: (*Off stage*) Ouch!

(*The* DIRECTOR, KOTRLÝ *and* FOUSTKA *look, surprised, at the bench.* NEUWIRTH *comes out of the bushes, holding his evidently injured ear, and moaning.*)

KOTRLÝ: What's happened, Alois?

NEUWIRTH: It's nothing . . .

DIRECTOR: What's wrong with your ear? Have you hurt it?

(NEUWIRTH *nods.*)

KOTRLÝ: Did something bite you?

(NEUWIRTH *nods, motioning with his head in the direction of the bushes from which he had come and out of which he is now followed by an embarrassed* PETRUŠKA. *She is nervously rearranging her costume and hair. The* DIRECTOR *and* KOTRLÝ *exchange significant glances and smile.* NEUWIRTH, *holding his ear and moaning, shuffles off to the right and disappears.* PETRUŠKA *shyly flits across the stage to the refreshments table and, her hand shaking a little, pours herself a drink, which she hurriedly drinks. The* DIRECTOR *and* KOTRLÝ *are about to leave.*)

FOUSTKA: Oh, Director . . .
(*The* DIRECTOR *and* KOTRLÝ *stop.*)

DIRECTOR: Yes, what is it, Doctor Foustka?
(*The* DEPUTY *enters, left. He does not at first see* PETRUŠKA, *who is hidden behind* FOUSTKA.)

DEPUTY: Have you seen Petruška?
(PETRUŠKA *comes up to the* DEPUTY, *smiles at him and takes his hand; from now on they will hold hands as before.*)
Where have you been, sweetheart?
(PETRUŠKA *whispers in the* DEPUTY's *ear. He listens attentively, then nods contentedly. The* DIRECTOR *and* KOTRLÝ *are about to leave.*)

FOUSTKA: Oh, Director . . .
(*The* DIRECTOR *and* KOTRLÝ *stop.*)

DIRECTOR: Yes, what is it, Doctor Foustka?

FOUSTKA: I'm sorry, I know you have a lot of other things on your mind, but on the other hand . . . I really must . . . having learned my lesson, I want to make sure nothing is neglected . . . I have made certain discoveries, which I have written down in my report . . .
(FOUSTKA *searches his pockets, looking for a piece of paper. The* DIRECTOR *and the* DEPUTY *exchange significant glances and come forward, still holding* KOTRLÝ *and* PETRUŠKA *by the hand. All four form a semi-circle centre stage around* FOUSTKA. *A short pause.*)

DIRECTOR: Don't bother . . .
(FOUSTKA *looks up, surprised, first at the* DIRECTOR, *then at the others. A tense pause.*)

FOUSTKA: But I thought . . .

(*Another tense pause, broken by the* DIRECTOR.)

DIRECTOR: (*In severe tones*) I'm not interested in what you
thought, I'm not interested in your piece of paper, I'm not
interested in you. You see, my dear sir, the comedy is over.

FOUSTKA: I don't understand . . . what comedy?

DIRECTOR: I'm afraid you have been too clever by half, and you
have badly underestimated us, taking us for much greater
idiots than we really are . . .

DEPUTY: You still don't understand?

FOUSTKA: No, I don't.

DIRECTOR: All right, then, I'll give it to you straight. We of
course knew all along what you thought of us, we knew that
you were merely pretending to be loyal while concealing
your true views and interests. Nevertheless, we decided to
give you one last chance and so we pretended to believe
your fairy-tale about working for us undercover, so to
speak. We were curious to see how you would conduct
yourself after the scare we gave you, whether perhaps you
might at last see the error of your ways and come to your
senses. And what did you do? You chose to spit at our
helping hand, and by so doing you have sealed your fate.

FOUSTKA: That's not true!

DIRECTOR: You know only too well that it is.

FOUSTKA: I suppose you can prove it?

DIRECTOR: (*To the* DEPUTY) Shall we oblige?

DEPUTY: I'd say yes. Let's.

(*The* DIRECTOR *puts two fingers in his mouth and gives a
piercing whistle.* FISTULA, *who has all this time been hidden
in the summer-house, jumps out of his hiding place.* FOUSTKA
sees him and grows agitated. FISTULA *quickly limps towards
the* DIRECTOR.)

FISTULA: Yes, boss, what can I do for you?

DIRECTOR: What did Foustka tell you yesterday?

FISTULA: He said he would pretend to be working undercover
for you, while in fact, in cahoots with those you're fighting
against, sabotaging your intelligence service at every step.
He said, and I quote, that he would be our – that is, *their* –

agent in the very midst of the enemy . . .

FOUSTKA: (*Shouts*) He's lying!

DIRECTOR: What did you say? Can you repeat that?

FOUSTKA: I said he was lying.

DIRECTOR: How dare you? How dare you insinuate that one of my finest external collaborators and a personal friend of long standing is a liar. Fistula *never* lies to us!

DEPUTY: Just what I was about to say, Director, Fistula *never* lies to us!

(LORENCOVÁ *and the* SECRETARY *enter, left, at the same time as the* LOVERS, *all four having left the dance-floor; both couples are holding hands. They join the others, inconspicuously enlarging the semi-circle around* FOUSTKA.)

FOUSTKA: (*To* FISTULA) So I fell into your trap, after all, didn't I?

FISTULA: I'm sorry, Doctor . . . (*To the* DIRECTOR) He still has his title, does he?

DIRECTOR: Oh, fuck all that . . .

FISTULA: Well, I'm sorry, Henry, but here you go again – simplifying everything. Did I not let you know all along that you had a range of choices and that you alone could decide your fate? You did not fall into any trap of mine, you came a cropper thanks to your own pride, which led you to believe that you could play both ends against the middle and get away with it. Have you forgotten the pains I took to explain to you that man has to respect *someone* in authority – whoever that someone may be – unless he wants to come to a bad end? And that even revolution has its rules? Did I say that or didn't I? I really cannot see how I could have made things any clearer to you. So my conscience is clear . . . I did what I could. I'm afraid it's your funeral if you failed to understand . . .

DIRECTOR: As always, Fistula is absolutely right. You simply cannot serve all masters, and at the same time deceive them all. You can't just take and give nothing in return. Every one of us has to decide where he stands.

DEPUTY: Just what I was about to say, Director. Every one of us has to decide where he stands.

(*The music grows noticeably louder – we again hear the tango as before.* VILMA *and the* DANCER *come running in, having left the dance-floor. They run through the semi-circle around* FOUSTKA *to centre stage, where they again execute some complicated tango steps, the* DANCER *bending* VILMA *right over so that the top of her head almost brushes the ground. The music again grows softer, and* VILMA *and the* DANCER, *holding hands like all the other couples, join the semi-circle.*)

FOUSTKA: Isn't it paradoxical that now when I have finally lost and my knowledge can serve no purpose, I'm beginning to understand it all. Fistula is right: I am a conceited idiot who thought he could use the devil without having to sign his soul away to him. As if the devil could be deceived.

FISTULA: Hold on a minute! Just hold on there. I never said that there is such a thing as the devil!

FOUSTKA: That's as maybe – but I'm saying it. And he's right here among us!

FISTULA: I see – you mean me, of course?

FOUSTKA: Hardly. You're just a subordinate little demon.

DIRECTOR: I know the way your mind works, Foustka, and I see that, through me, you would like to point an accusing finger at modern science and denounce it as the true source of all evil. Am I right?

FOUSTKA: No, you're not. Through you I merely wish to denounce the arrogance of intolerant, self-regarding power, which uses science as a handy bow with which to shoot down anything that threatens it. That is to say, anything which does not owe its authority to that power, or stems from some authority outside.

DIRECTOR: Is that the legacy you wish to leave the world, Foustka?

FOUSTKA: Yes!

DIRECTOR: Somewhat banal, wouldn't you say? In countries where they don't believe in censorship, any sports reporter worth his salt scatters such pearls of wisdom by the wayside. However, a legacy is a legacy, so let me demonstrate how tolerant I am – despite what others may think of me – by overlooking my objections and applauding you.

134

(*The* DIRECTOR *starts to clap, the others join in, one by one. At the same time the music grows more insistent – a piece of hard rock, wild and throbbing. If possible, the music should be composed so ingeniously that this would be a variation on the themes played before the performance and during the intervals, so that there is a connection between the stormy finale and the earlier music. The clapping soon turns rhythmical, in time to the music, which grows in volume until it is almost deafening. All those present, except* FOUSTKA, *gradually succumb to the rhythm – first they just move slightly in tune with the music, then they sway from side to side, until they are all dancing – at first each on his or her own, then in pairs, finally all together. The dance grows wilder all the time, until it turns into an orgiastic carnival.* FOUSTKA *takes no part in the dance, merely stumbling around among the dancers, who bump into him and disorientate him, so that he is unable to extricate himself from the mêlée, though it is obvious that he would like to.* KOTRLÝ *has left the stage, and now he returns, carrying a large bowl which has a flame burning in it. With this in his hands, he makes his difficult way through the dancers, until at last he manages to reach the summer-house, where he puts down the bowl. As he goes, however, he sets fire to* FOUSTKA'S *coat, so that a new chaotic element is added to the scene as* FOUSTKA, *his clothing on fire, runs to and fro in panic. Then, out of the summer-house where* KOTRLÝ *has placed his bowl, come thick, sulphurous fumes. The music thunders, the stage is completely obscured by smoke. As far as technically possible, the smoke invades the auditorium. After a while the music stops, the auditorium lights come on, and the audience sees that the curtain has come down in the meantime. There is a short silence, then music is heard again – this time softly and the most banal muzak. If the smoke, or the play itself, has not driven the last spectator out of the theatre, and if there is anyone left to applaud, the first to take a bow will be a fireman in uniform, with a helmet on his head and holding a fire extinguisher.*)

REDEVELOPMENT
or
SLUM CLEARANCE

English version by
JAMES SAUNDERS

from a literal translation by
Marie Winn

Redevelopment was first performed at the Orange Tree,
Richmond, on 7 September 1990. The cast was as follows:

PLEKHANOV	Frank Shelley
RENATA	Mairead Carty
ULCH	David Timson
LUISA	Janet Key
FIRST DELEGATE	Chris Tajah
SECOND DELEGATE	John Griffiths
ALBERT	Timothy Watson
ZDENEK BERGMAN	Tim Hardy
SPECIAL SECRETARY	Neale Goodrum
MRS MACOURKOVA	Isobil Nisbet
FIRST INSPECTOR	Chris Tajah
SECOND INSPECTOR	John Griffiths
THE WOMAN	Isobil Nisbet
Directed by	Sam Walters
Designed by	Mark Bailey

CHARACTERS

ZDENEK BERGMAN, Principal Project Director, fifty-ish
LUISA, architect, about forty
ALBERT, architect, about twenty-five
KUZMA PLEKHANOV, architect (male)
ULCH, architect
MRS MACOURKOVA, architect
RENATA, secretary, about twenty
SPECIAL SECRETARY
FIRST INSPECTOR
SECOND INSPECTOR
FIRST DELEGATE
SECOND DELEGATE
FIRST WOMAN
SECOND WOMAN

SET

The play is set entirely in the spacious hall of a medieval castle somewhere in Czechoslovakia. Around and beneath the castle – it stands on an eminence – lies the ancient town which it once ruled. It is to prepare a plan for the redevelopment of this town that a team of architects is now quartered in the castle, their workrooms in the castle chambers.

On the right-hand side of the hall three steps lead to a massive door to the outside world (right door); along the left-hand wall is a stairway with a little balustrade which is interrupted about a yard above ground level by a landing giving access to a door in the left wall (left door). The stairway then continues to a gallery running the whole length of the rear wall, forming in effect a second floor. There are two doors giving on to the gallery (left upper door and right upper door). On the ground floor, in the rear wall beneath the gallery, are two more doors (left rear door and right rear door). There are thus six doors – one to the outside, the others to other parts of the castle.

In the centre of the hall, parallel to the front of the stage, is a great Gothic table surrounded by eight high Gothic chairs. Other chairs of various kinds, and perhaps some little tables and chests, are placed around the walls and in the corners. On the walls, together with a number of old painted portraits, are pinned architectural plans, sketches and photographs. In the middle of the central table stands a large model, in polystyrene, of a hill with a modern village at its foot and up its sides, and a Gothic castle on the summit.

ACT I

*A violin is playing the well-known Russian song 'Ochi Cherniya'.
The lights go up to reveal the player:* PLEKHANOV, *alone on stage,
wearing a dressing-gown and carpet slippers, his dress throughout the
play. He is completely absorbed in the playing, humming
spasmodically to himself. After some moments* RENATA *enters by the
left door and stands on the landing waiting for him to stop. Pause.*

RENATA: Excuse me, sir.

    (PLEKHANOV *doesn't hear. Pause.*)

    (*Louder*) Mr Plekhanov, sir –

    (PLEKHANOV *doesn't hear. Pause.*)

    Excuse me, sir!

    (PLEKHANOV *stops playing and looks across at her.*)

PLEKHANOV: Are you talking to me?

RENATA: The Director requests that if you must play you play
    something more cheerful.

    (PLEKHANOV *stops playing and puts his fiddle down.* ULCH
    *appears at the upper right door. He wears, throughout the play,
    a white lab. coat.* RENATA *is leaving by the left door.*)

ULCH: Renata . . .

    (RENATA *stops, hesitates for a moment, then turns to* ULCH.)

RENATA: May I help you?

ULCH: Would you have a moment?

RENATA: I'm sorry, Mr Ulch, but –

ULCH: It is important.

RENATA: I have work to do.

ULCH: We all have work to do. Please –

RENATA: I really can't just now.

    (RENATA *turns quickly and goes out by the left door, leaving
    *ULCH *gazing after her. Pause.*)

PLEKHANOV: A mind of her own.

    (ULCH *goes out through the right upper door, as* LUISA *enters
    by the left upper door and looks over the balustrade at
    *PLEKHANOV.)

LUISA: Kuzma, why aren't you playing?
  (LUISA *comes slowly down the stairs*.)
PLEKHANOV: Chief doesn't like it.
LUISA: He must be having another of his bad times.
PLEKHANOV: Problems for you again, eh?
LUISA: Hm.
PLEKHANOV: Have you tried keeping him emotionally
  occupied?
LUISA: How do you mean?
PLEKHANOV: I don't know – pretend to be unfaithful – or
  jealous – suddenly overwhelm him with tenderness – or
  disgust . . .
  (*A dog begins to bark wildly outside.* PLEKHANOV *and* LUISA
  *glance across at the right door. The barking stops after a
  moment, and there is a knock on the door*.)
LUISA: Come in!
  (*Through the right door enter the* FIRST *and* SECOND
  DELEGATES. *The* FIRST DELEGATE *is black. They come down
  the steps and pause*.)
FIRST DELEGATE: Good afternoon.
SECOND DELEGATE: – noon.
  (*Pause*.)
LUISA: Can I help you?
FIRST DELEGATE: We'd like to see the Project Director, please.
SECOND DELEGATE: Director, please.
LUISA: I'll see if he's free.
  (LUISA *begins to mount the stairs to the left door. On the
  landing she stops and turns*.)
  Who shall I say?
FIRST DELEGATE: We represent the citizens.
SECOND DELEGATE: –tizens.
  (LUISA *and* PLEKHANOV *exchange a curious glance*.)
LUISA: Right.
  (*She goes out.* PLEKHANOV *picks up his fiddle and shuffles
  towards the right rear door. He stops to look at them*.)
PLEKHANOV: You're looking at my dressing-gown.
FIRST DELEGATE: No no.
SECOND DELEGATE: No.

144

(PLEKHANOV *shuffles out. Pause. The* DELEGATES *look around.* ALBERT *enters by the left door and comes downstairs quickly.*)

FIRST DELEGATE: Afternoon.

SECOND DELEGATE: – noon.

ALBERT: Good afternoon.

FIRST DELEGATE: Are you the Project Director?

ALBERT: Sorry.

FIRST DELEGATE: Sorry.

SECOND DELEGATE: Sorry.

ALBERT: No no.

(ALBERT *hurries out of the left rear door. Pause. The* DELEGATES *look round.* BERGMAN *enters through the left door and walks slowly down towards the* DELEGATES.)

FIRST DELEGATE: Good afternoon.

SECOND DELEGATE: – noon.

(BERGMAN *shakes their hands, motions them to take a seat, and sits himself at the left end of the table. The* DELEGATES *remain standing. Short pause.*)

BERGMAN: What can I do for you?

FIRST DELEGATE: Are you the Project Director?

BERGMAN: Yes.

FIRST DELEGATE: We represent the two hundred and sixteen residents who signed this, erm . . .

(*He nudges the* SECOND DELEGATE, *who pulls a folded sheet of paper from his pocket.*)

SECOND DELEGATE: Signed this . . . (*Begins to read:*) 'As permanent residents of the town, we the undersigned wish to record our disapproval of the plans for redevelopment. We do not wish to live in temporary accommodation for an indefinite number of years and then return to an environment that has nothing to do with our former home. We understand that the purpose of the scheme is to improve our living conditions and health standards, but we have lived contentedly for many decades in the timeless atmosphere of this picturesque and historically unique castle town, and do not want it changed. We should be very unhappy to have our present homes taken away.'

FIRST DELEGATE: Signed, you see, by two hundred and sixteen citizens . . .

SECOND DELEGATE: –tizens.

(*Longer pause.*)

BERGMAN: You know, this is a serious matter . . .

FIRST DELEGATE: Oh yes.

BERGMAN: I understand your position.

FIRST DELEGATE: Good.

BERGMAN: It's only natural, from your point of view . . .

FIRST DELEGATE: We're glad you think so . . .

SECOND DELEGATE: Think so.

BERGMAN: But why are you coming to me?

FIRST DELEGATE: Well, you're in charge of the project!

BERGMAN: My dear chap, I may be in charge *here*; but it's not my brief to make judgements on the work assigned us, or change it at will. My concern is that we discharge our responsibilities as well as we can within the given parameters which –

(*He stops as the* SPECIAL SECRETARY *enters through the left upper door, comes quickly downstairs and approaches the* SECOND DELEGATE. *The* SPECIAL SECRETARY *walks quite noiselessly, except for one of his shoes which squeaks loudly.*)

SPECIAL SECRETARY: May I, if you please . . .?

(*He takes the paper from the* SECOND DELEGATE, *reads it, studies it, turns it over. Then he looks searchingly at the* SECOND DELEGATE.)

Who wrote this for you?

FIRST DELEGATE: We did . . .

SPECIAL SECRETARY: You didn't say that very convincingly.

(*Pause.*)

Well? Who then?

FIRST DELEGATE: We wrote it ourselves, really.

SECOND DELEGATE: Really.

SPECIAL SECRETARY: How do you mean, 'we'? All together? On the same pen? Is that what you mean?

FIRST DELEGATE: Everyone who signed stands behind it . . .

SPECIAL SECRETARY: I'm not asking who stands behind it or underneath it or on top of it, I'm asking who wrote it.

146

(*Pause.*)

Well, if you won't say, you won't say!

(*He walks round the table, absorbed in thought. Then he perches on the corner of the table nearest the* DELEGATES *and stares fixedly at them.*)

I understand that two thousand people live in the town. Two thousand souls, as they used to call them, crammed into small, dark, cold, damp houses with totally inadequate toilet facilities and a derisory number of baths, a source of poverty, suffering and infection. What a relic of the old social order, when the lords lived here in the castle and their subjects, their souls, down in the town. What a sad heritage. This project is not just for you, you know, it's for the good of us all!

(*Pause.*)

So?

FIRST DELEGATE: So?

SECOND DELEGATE: So?

SPECIAL SECRETARY: Will you withdraw it?

FIRST DELEGATE: We don't have the right to do that . . .

SECOND DELEGATE: The right.

SPECIAL SECRETARY: As you wish.

(*He stands up, folds the paper and pockets it, then walks round the table absorbed in thought and stops again in front of the* DELEGATES.)

How many did you say signed it?

FIRST DELEGATE: Two hundred and sixteen . . .

SECOND DELEGATE: –teen.

SPECIAL SECRETARY: About 10 per cent! And did you ask the remaining 90 per cent for their opinion?

FIRST DELEGATE: All sorts of people signed: a cross-section, different classes, different races . . . We all feel the same way . . .

SPECIAL SECRETARY: So why didn't everybody sign it? No, no, my friends, it's clear to me that these are the tactics of a pressure group, a minority pretending to speak for the majority! You won't withdraw it?

FIRST DELEGATE: No . . .

SECOND DELEGATE: No.

SPECIAL SECRETARY: Your mistake . . .

(*He turns and runs out through the left door.*)

FIRST DELEGATE: Who was that?

BERGMAN: The Special Secretary.

FIRST DELEGATE: Ah. We'd better be going . . .

BERGMAN: Just a moment . . .

FIRST DELEGATE: Yes?

BERGMAN: I don't know if this will make you feel any better, but let me say something. First: building facilities are non-existent at present, and probably will be for the foreseeable future. All we're doing is making studies. In other words, don't cross your bridges before they're built. Second: we're not barbarians. Our studies are carried out with one factor in mind: the unique spirit and needs of the particular locality we're dealing with. Why do you think we've come here and not stayed in the studio the way they usually do? We asked to be moved here so that we could breathe in the local atmosphere, get to know you, learn your preferences at first hand, your habits, your roots and ties, to wander through your winding little streets, admire your gardens, catch the scent of the rose-covered porches, peer into your wells . . . to live your kind of life, in your midst, and armed with this experience to produce something which would neither sacrifice your past nor . . . betray your future . . .

FIRST DELEGATE: Thank you.

BERGMAN: My pleasure.

(ALBERT *enters through the left rear door and hurries towards the staircase.*)

FIRST DELEGATE: We'll be off then. *Ciao.*

SECOND DELEGATE: *Ciao.*

BERGMAN: *Ciao.*

(*The* DELEGATES *exit through the right door, as* LUISA, *a cup of coffee in each hand, enters through the left door.* ALBERT *stops suddenly at the staircase and steps back to let* LUISA *past, who, as she passes, smiles at him.* ALBERT, *embarrassed, runs up the stairs and out through the left upper door.* LUISA *puts one coffee in front of* BERGMAN *and keeps one for herself. They sit stirring their coffees, which they will drink as they talk. Pause.*)

LUISA: How are you feeling?

BERGMAN: I think I'm going to put an end to it.

LUISA: To what?

BERGMAN: Everything!

LUISA: Seriously, Zdenek . . .

BERGMAN: I'm dead serious.

LUISA: What's the matter?

BERGMAN: Nothing. Except that I despise myself, I hate myself, I'm sick of myself . . .

LUISA: I get sick of myself sometimes, but that's no reason to – !

BERGMAN: I'm so averse to life I go to bed before I'm tired and force myself to stay asleep in the morning; at least sleep is a kind of substitute for the non-existence I crave. Every night before I drop off I make a wish, that I won't wake up in the morning, that everything will be over, finished!

LUISA: You mustn't talk like that!

BERGMAN: I've become incapable of getting pleasure out of anything, can't you see it written in the lines of my face? My life is nothing but a tiresome duty, a source of endless suffering. Which I then inflict on others, you above all. What's the sense in living a life that's lost its sense? Darkness, peace, eternal, endless, absolute peace . . .

LUISA: Stop it, that's enough! You really are a charlatan, you know!

BERGMAN: I'm being absolutely sincere . . .

LUISA: You're only saying all this because you need someone to pity you. Someone to console you, flatter you, worry about you; despair over you. It's just attention-seeking: you're trying to involve other people in your problems so as to find a kind of self-justification in their anxiety, some external proof that you actually exist. The fact is, you exploit everybody around you! You're like a spoilt child! (*Pause.*)

BERGMAN: Luisa . . .

149

LUISA: What?

BERGMAN: A beautiful woman like you, desirable, good-hearted
– you could easily find someone else to be happy with.
Someone you admired. Why don't you?

LUISA: You see! That's what I mean!

BERGMAN: What is?

LUISA: Just what I'm talking about! You said that purely and
simply to get me to fall on my knees and cry through my
tears that I can't live without you!

BERGMAN: You think that's what I'm after? Cheap melodrama?

LUISA: You'd love it! The cheaper the better!

BERGMAN: Luisa, if your Freudian interpretations explained my
condition I'd be only too happy. But it's deeper than that.
It's not a psychological problem! It's metaphysical! I don't
need self-justification, I need meaning! But of course you
love that kind of simple diagnosis; then you can write out a
simple prescription: take no notice and it'll go away!
(*Pause*.)
(*Quietly*) Luisa . . .

LUISA: Hm?

BERGMAN: Don't you at least feel now and then . . . just a tiny
bit sorry for me?

LUISA: Now and then . . . a tiny bit.

BERGMAN: Luisa . . .

LUISA: Come to me then . . . There, there . . . There,
there . . .
(BERGMAN *sinks to his knees in front of* LUISA, *embracing her,
pressing his head to her lap.* LUISA *strokes his head pensively.*
RENATA *enters by the left door. On the landing she stops, looks
down as if she wants to speak but, seeing* BERGMAN *at*
LUISA'*s feet, decides to leave. However,* ULCH *has appeared at
the right upper door.*)

ULCH: Renata . . .
(RENATA *stops, hesitates, then turns to* ULCH. *At the sound of*
ULCH'*s voice* BERGMAN *gets up quickly and returns to
normal.*)

RENATA: May I help you?

ULCH: Would you have a moment?

150

RENATA: I have work to do, Mr Ulch –
ULCH: We all have work to do. Please . . .
RENATA: I really can't just now.

> (RENATA *goes out quickly by the left door.* ULCH's *eyes follow her.* PLEKHANOV *appears, carrying his fiddle, at the right rear door. He stands in the doorway, and begins to play softly a lyrical tune.*)

ULCH: A mind of her own!

> (*The lights go down, but the music continues through the intermission.*)

ACT II

The stage is empty, but the music may still be heard playing; but it presently stops, as RENATA *and* LUISA *enter by the left rear door.* RENATA *is carrying seven plates,* LUISA *has napkins and tableware. They go to the table and begin to lay it.*

RENATA: So you think it's all right, Luisa?

LUISA: It depends on the circumstances. For instance, you're less likely to do it with someone if you're in love with someone else than if you're on your own, or in a long-term relationship. And obviously it's easier with someone who attracts you than with someone you find revolting. Then you have to take into account your moral values and how strong they are, whether it's momentary lust or a matter of life and death, and so on. It's complicated . . .

RENATA: I couldn't do it with someone I didn't love!

LUISA: Don't be too sure! Still, I hope so for your sake! You'll have fewer problems that way . . .

RENATA: We've laid one too many again.

LUISA: You, me, Ulch, Plekhanov, Albert, Bergman . . . Mrs Macourkova.

RENATA: I always forget Mrs Macourkova.

(RENATA *and* LUISA *finish laying the table and go out through the left rear door.* ULCH *appears at the right upper door, sees nobody, and disappears again.* RENATA *and* LUISA *enter through the left rear door,* RENATA *with several bottles of beer,* LUISA *carrying a tray of glasses and bottle openers. These they lay out on the table.*)

Is it true that if two people do it who don't love each other, she's more likely to fall in love with him afterwards than he is with her?

LUISA: Well, you know, a woman looks for stability, something solid and permanent; her sights tend to be set on home and family, so any liaison is seen as a possible relationship . . .

RENATA: I'm not sure I could do it even with someone I *was* in love with.

LUISA: How gorgeously innocent you are! Don't worry, Renata, when you're really in love it'll happen and you won't even know how. All at once it will seem so obvious, so simple, so natural and so pure . . .

(*They finish laying the table and go out by the left rear door. ULCH appears at the right rear door, sees nobody and disappears again. RENATA and LUISA enter through the left rear door, RENATA with a pot of goulash and a ladle, LUISA with a basket of rolls.*)

(*Calls out*) Dinner!

(*They set down the pot and the basket; RENATA passes LUISA the plates, into which LUISA ladles the goulash. Meanwhile the others enter: ULCH from the right upper door, then PLEKHANOV with his fiddle through the right rear door; then ALBERT through the left rear door, and finally BERGMAN through the left door. BERGMAN sits in his chair at the left end of the table, after which the others sit down. RENATA opens the bottles and pours beer for the others; then she and LUISA sit down. A pause: they look towards BERGMAN, who is far away. He comes to himself, realizing that the others are waiting for him.*)

BERGMAN: Sorry . . . Well – *bon appetit!*

ALL: *Bon appetit!*

(*They begin to eat. Pause. MACOURKOVA enters by the left rear door and hurries to her seat.*)

MACOURKOVA: I'm so sorry . . .

(*She sits down quickly and begins to eat. Pause.*)

PLEKHANOV: Do you know there's an interesting legend about this castle? I discovered it today in the library . . .

LUISA: A ghost story, I hope.

PLEKHANOV: A certain countess, the wife of an ancient lord of the castle, fell madly in love with her groom . . .

LUISA: Oh, a love story . . .

PLEKHANOV: Listen. As a result, they say, the count's ghost wreaks his revenge on any man in love who enters his walls . . .

153

LUISA: How does he do that?

PLEKHANOV: By throwing him off the tower, into the moat.

ULCH: Every castle has its legends. I've heard better.

PLEKHANOV: The last count was in fact found dead in the moat; the older people down there still remember it. Though since it happened the day before he had his marching orders, other explanations do present themselves.

ULCH: When we convert the moat to a swimming pool it'll put a damper on that story.

PLEKHANOV: I take these legends with a pinch of salt, but I must admit I sense in the tower a certain – ambience.

LUISA: You spend your life sensing ambiences, Kuzma. Stop trying to scare us!

ULCH: I have an idea! For that two-storey building in Zone Two of the Public Utilities! Next to the Children's Play Area! A permanent exhibition on superstition and prejudice! To gently indoctrinate children into the scientific approach so that –

(*He stops. The* SPECIAL SECRETARY *enters by the right upper door, crosses the gallery and descends the stairs.*)

MACOURKOVA: Good evening, Secretary!

SPECIAL SECRETARY: Good evening, Mrs –

MACOURKOVA: Macourkova. Why don't you ever dine with us? It would be jolly!

SPECIAL SECRETARY: Do you think so?

(*He crosses to the right door and goes out. Pause.*)

PLEKHANOV: Why is it, do you think, that only one of the Special Secretary's shoes squeaks?

(*A slightly embarrassed titter.*)

ALBERT: What did the men want?

BERGMAN: Hm? What men?

ALBERT: The men from down there.

BERGMAN: Oh, they're opposed to the redevelopment. They think we want to take their homes away.

ULCH: Typical of those people! If we took their attitude into account nothing would ever be built! Civilization would become moribund!

(*Slight pause.*)

154

ALBERT: What did you tell them?

BERGMAN: What could *I* tell them? The Special Secretary had a word with them. He called it the tactics of a pressure group.
(*Slight pause.*)

ULCH: If you ask me we're being cackhanded about the whole thing.

BERGMAN: Cackhanded about what?

ULCH: Hidden away up here, making our plans, nobody knows what they are . . . Naturally they get wild ideas . . .

BERGMAN: And how do you think we *should* go about it? Run down and get their approval for every sketch we do?

ULCH: No no. But for instance, if we organized a series of popular lectures to explain to them, in terms they could understand, how much nicer it'll be once they've got central heating, a decent House of Culture, a Central Laundry, Refuse Disposal . . . they'd begin to see that our sole aim is to enhance the quality of their lives. I dare say most of them haven't the faintest idea they're still living in the last century!

ALBERT: I'm sorry – !

ULCH: You disagree? I thought you'd like the idea.

ALBERT: I'm sorry, but you're making those people out to be stupid. Do you think they've never seen a modern housing project?

ULCH: I dare say they have, but all they see –

ALBERT: And you're surprised that we terrify them? I'd be surprised if we didn't!

ULCH: Albert, I realize that some uninformed laymen like to write off the whole of modern architecture on the basis of one or two less-than-perfect examples, which I admit do exist, but as far as I know you are a qualified architect –

LUISA: He didn't say he agrees with them. Only that he's not surprised at them.

ULCH: I don't see the difference!

ALBERT: Look, I'm not against new buildings *per se* –

ULCH: Then what are you saying? That we should use medieval methods to build them?

ALBERT: We couldn't if we tried. We wouldn't know how.

ULCH: Who needs to? Things have changed, Albert, since your grandfather's time. And I'm not just talking about prefabrication and synthetic materials –

ALBERT: What then? What's changed?

ULCH: Good Lord, what did you do at college, Albert? Generations of the finest architectural minds have spent their genius on the concept of the city of the future; we're the cutting edge of all that. We know how to design the ideal living environment, aesthetically pleasing but structurally coherent, a smoothly running complex of efficient communication systems, state-of-the-art commercial networks, parks, rest areas and entertainment zones. And you think we should leave them to live in holes in the ground for the sake of a feudal past!

ALBERT: It's what they tried to teach me at college that makes me understand those people down there!

ULCH: Elucidate, Albert, elucidate.

ALBERT: What they know better than us down there is how complicated things can get in your ideal city. It needs more than planning!

ULCH: So in your opinion urban renewal is bunkum –

ALBERT: I'm not saying that! I'm saying that cities worth living in are like part of nature, they need to develop over the centuries, they're the result of – how can I explain it? – generations of experience, quietly collected and handed down – people's feelings, evolving historically, anonymous people, people with a sense of humility in the face of everything that seems beyond their understanding, their . . .

ULCH: In the face of what? Can you be specific?

ALBERT: I'm talking about their respect for the character of the countryside, the laws of nature, the legacy their ancestors left them, that beauty of form that comes of different kinds of people living together over a long period of –

ULCH: But, bloody hell, we –

PLEKHANOV: Please! Let him finish what he's saying. (*To* ALBERT) Do go on.

ALBERT: I've finished. I'm only worried at the idea of sweeping everything away like a load of old rubbish and replacing it with a mental concept. None of us has a formula for universal happiness, and we have no right to overturn people's lives as if we had . . .

ULCH: Who was it suggested organizing lectures and discussion groups?

ALBERT: What's the good of discussions when you've already decided you're right and they're wrong? You may feel superior, I don't! Not when I think of that hideous housing project out there, you know the one, they do anyway; ruined countryside all round. You say 'less than perfect', as if that kind of thing is a sort of oversight. It's not, it's the logical end product of the conceit of architects who think they understand how life works. If you want an example of your ideal living environment why not be honest and use a battery chicken farm!

ULCH: Coffee-house philosophy. Very trendy, Albert, but like most trendy ideas not very original. Every conservative reactionary in the country spouts that stuff, it's their stock in trade. Return to the past, respect tradition, etc., etc. Forget about scientific and technological progress, pretend micro-electronics and space rockets don't exist. We live in a global civilization, Albert, with all the enormous problems that come with it, not least the population explosion; and you want us to abandon everything and leave the world to its fate!

ALBERT: You can't solve everything in your mind! That's all I'm saying. You can't. If you want proof, look at this modern world you're so fond of. We're laying it waste in the name of progress! We're not improving life, we're manipulating it to death!

ULCH: Oh, bravo!

ALBERT: I don't think it's a laughing matter.

ULCH: I'm sorry. So what do you recommend?

ALBERT: It's obvious, isn't it? Adaptability – humility – respect for human standards, for life at its own level – respect for

its diversity, its unpredictability, its mystery . . .
Respect . . .

(*A short, rather embarrassed pause. Then they all turn to* BERGMAN.)

BERGMAN: May I break in here? I'm glad to hear the various viewpoints expressed so sharply and – forcefully. It makes for a lively debate, and that can lead to something. Personally, I found what was said most useful: it makes me realize with renewed urgency the purpose of our mission here: not to force on the people our private utopias – which luckily we have no capacity to carry out at present; neither, though, to abandon our expertise and rely on tradition and the spontaneous creativity of the anonymous masses to solve today's complex problems of urban existence for us. The only way left, then, is to seek out with incisiveness but sensitivity such architectonic solutions as may be in harmony with the tasks, demands and possibilities of the time, and with the natural and basically unpredictable diversity of life. In other words, I'm for progress, Ulch; but progress, Albert, with a human face. (*To* MACOURKOVA) What is your opinion on this, Mrs Macourkova?

MACOURKOVA: Oh, well, you know . . .

(*She shrugs her shoulders uncertainly.*)

BERGMAN: Yes . . .

(*He gets up, nods slightly to the others and leaves, up the stairs to the left door. The others also get up. While* RENATA *and* LUISA *begin to clear the table* ULCH *goes upstairs to the gallery. Picking up his fiddle,* PLEKHANOV *strums a chord on it, and slaps* ALBERT *enthusiastically on the back.*)

PLEKHANOV: Good, Albert! Very good!

(ALBERT, *whose eyes were on* LUISA, *is embarrassed.* PLEKHANOV *goes out by the right rear door as the* SPECIAL SECRETARY *comes in by the left rear door, and makes for the stairs.*)

MACOURKOVA: Secretary!

SPECIAL SECRETARY: Mrs . . .

MACOURKOVA: Macourkova! You seem so busy; I hope you're
    sleeping well!
SPECIAL SECRETARY: Very well. Good night.
MACOURKOVA: Sweet dreams!

*(The SPECIAL SECRETARY nods, goes downstairs to the left
door and exits. RENATA and LUISA leave by the left rear door
carrying some of the dishes, etc. MACOURKOVA follows them
out through the same door. ULCH, on the gallery, looks down at
ALBERT.)*

ULCH: Given your views, I wonder you ever joined this
    profession.
ALBERT: When there's a threat to life, someone's got to protect
    it!
ULCH: You're not protecting life. You're protecting never-never
    land. Good night.

*(ULCH goes out by the left upper door. RENATA and LUISA
come in again by the left rear door. RENATA glances across at
ALBERT, who is, however, gazing at LUISA. RENATA and
LUISA clear the rest of the table.)*

ALBERT: Do you need any help?
LUISA: Thanks, Albert, we can manage.

*(RENATA and LUISA go out by the left rear door with the
remainder of the dishes, as the SPECIAL SECRETARY enters by
the left upper door. Coming downstairs, he walks towards the
right rear door.)*

ALBERT: Secretary!
SPECIAL SECRETARY: *(Stopping)* What is it?
ALBERT: Where are they?
SPECIAL SECRETARY: Who?
ALBERT: Those people's representatives . . .
SPECIAL SECRETARY: Why does that interest you?
ALBERT: No particular reason . . .
SPECIAL SECRETARY: They're in custody.
ALBERT: You mean in the dungeon?
SPECIAL SECRETARY: Don't worry, they're not hungry there.
    But since you've mentioned it, I've a question for you.
ALBERT: Which is?

SPECIAL SECRETARY: You don't happen to know who wrote the petition for them?

ALBERT: No, why should I?

SPECIAL SECRETARY: Are you sure? Do try to remember.

ALBERT: I've told you, I don't know!

SPECIAL SECRETARY: Well, we shall see . . .

(*He squeaks out by the right rear door.* ALBERT, *thinking deeply, crosses to a chair and flops down in it.* RENATA *and* LUISA *come in by the left rear door.*)

LUISA: Good night then, Renata. Thanks for your help.

RENATA: Good night.

(RENATA *goes upstairs to the left door, but stops on the landing to glance at* ALBERT. *He doesn't notice, so she goes out by the left door.* LUISA *goes up to* ALBERT, *strokes his head and sits down beside him.*)

LUISA: That was quite a show you put on, Albert.

ALBERT: I let myself get carried away, it was stupid . . .

LUISA: It's good to hear *someone* around here saying what they feel.

ALBERT: Do you think there'll be trouble?

LUISA: Zdenek will fix it; I'll tell him.

ALBERT: Thank you.

(*Pause.*)

LUISA: I rather envy you . . .

ALBERT: Me? For goodness' sake, why?

LUISA: Your youth . . .

ALBERT: You talk as if you're old!

LUISA: I only mean you haven't been spoiled by the world yet; unlike the rest of us.

ALBERT: Not you!

LUISA: I'm not sure about that. I used to make speeches like that once upon a time. We all did . . .

ALBERT: Even Ulch?

LUISA: Even Ulch. His kind of speech, of course. But at least with real passion.

(*Pause.*)

ALBERT: I don't know what to do . . .

LUISA: Be yourself.

160

ALBERT: Whoever that is . . . Everything seems unreal to me –
this castle, the project, everyone here – I know exactly
what they're going to say, what they're going to do – It's as
if they're not people but characters in a play someone's
putting on –

LUISA: When life teaches *you* to be cautious, Albert, you'll also
learn to be more careful how you judge the rest of us . . .
Oh, forget I said that. You're quite right.

ALBERT: I wasn't including you!

LUISA: Why ever not?

ALBERT: You're different. There's something special about you
– if I got into trouble you'd be the one I'd come to . . .

LUISA: Like a mother?

ALBERT: God, no, I'm sorry, I didn't mean it like that!

LUISA: No need to apologize.
(*Pause.*)

ALBERT: They've put them in the dungeon! It's grotesque . . .

LUISA: Par for the course.

ALBERT: Can't something be done?

LUISA: I'll ask Zdenek.
(PLEKHANOV *appears at the right rear door, tuning his fiddle,
holding it to his ear. Neither* LUISA *nor* ALBERT *sees him.*
LUISA *stands up; then* ALBERT *also stands.*)
Don't look so agonized. Go to bed. Forget it. Here, come
here.
(*She kisses him on the forehead.*)
There. A motherly kiss goodnight.
(ALBERT *hesitates, then backs away in confusion towards the
left rear door.* LUISA, *smiling at him, waves; he waves back
awkwardly, and backs out of the left rear door as* PLEKHANOV
begins to play a lyrical tune. LUISA *looks up at him.*)
A nice lad, isn't he?

PLEKHANOV: Oh yes . . . He's in love with you.

LUISA: Do you think so?

PLEKHANOV: I'm never wrong about these things . . .
(*He begins to play more loudly as the lights go down.*)

ACT III

PLEKHANOV, *who has played throughout the intermission, is on stage with* ALBERT. *He plays for a few moments longer, then puts the fiddle down. Pause.*

ALBERT: Imagine, for instance, you've a momentous decision to make, two choices, A or B. You know choice A would be in your interest, but at the same time a certain voice tells you that the right thing to do is B –
(RENATA *enters by the left door, carrying a tray with two cups of coffee on it. She begins to climb the stairs but, hearing what* ALBERT *is saying, she stops and listens attentively.*)
It's only a voice in your own head, yet you have the feeling that *it*'s in charge of you, it seems to matter in some mysterious way. You want to do what it tells you; and even though you finally decide to do the other thing you at least try to explain why, defend yourself in front of it, get its approval. You must know what I'm talking about!
(RENATA *goes quickly out by the left upper door.* ULCH *looks out from the right upper door, just fails to see* RENATA, *and disappears again.*)
PLEKHANOV: Yes, go on. What about it?
ALBERT: Well, that mysterious inner voice – what can it be but the voice of the Supreme Being?
PLEKHANOV: I think it's a little more complicated than that, my friend –
(RENATA, *her tray empty, enters by the left upper door and descends the stairs. At the landing she stops again and listens.*)
ALBERT: Yes, I know I'm oversimplifying, but even so – I mean how would we know a thing was good if there weren't some kind of standard outside us? Our sense of goodness doesn't just come from ourselves. It's a sense of harmony with something that was here before us and will be here after us, something eternal. That's what I think. A harmony that

makes us – insignificant. I don't know how to talk about these things, but it seems so obvious to me . . .

RENATA: Oh, and to me! . . . Sorry!

(*She runs through the left door in confusion.* ALBERT *watches this in surprise. Slight pause.*)

PLEKHANOV: She's in love with you.

ALBERT: With me? Nonsense!

PLEKHANOV: I'm never wrong about these things. But to get back to your little sermon: for most of us, I'm afraid, that voice you talk about is no more than a faint dying whisper nowadays; hum a little tune to yourself and you drown it out completely. Yours won't make your life any easier, but I hope it lasts. Because I'll tell you this for what it's worth, Albert: the persistence of your inner voice may be the only thing keeping a certain fiddle-playing eccentric from the absolute conviction that everything is definitively and finally up shit creek.

(*He plucks a single disharmonious chord on his fiddle, pats* ALBERT *gently on the back and goes out by the right rear door, leaving* ALBERT *to ponder on this.* BERGMAN *and* LUISA *come in by the left door and come downstairs.*)

BERGMAN: Greetings, Albert. Ça va?

ALBERT: Good morning. Look, I, erm . . .

BERGMAN: Cooled down a little this morning?

ALBERT: I'm sorry about yesterday. I was – a little . . .

BERGMAN: No need for apologies, I'm not angry. But a word of friendly advice: it really would be advisable to express yourself a little more circumspectly, at least in front of some of our colleagues. There's nothing that can't be said, of course, we need the occasional gust of fresh air blowing through; but a little more strategy might better serve the interests of your cause, as well as your own. I'm sure you understand me.

ALBERT: Yes . . . Yes, of course . . .

(*A short embarrassed pause;* ALBERT *glances across at* LUISA, *who smiles at him.*)

Well, I'll erm . . .

(*He exits by the left rear door.* BERGMAN *and* LUISA *sit down.*)

BERGMAN: We're going to have complications over him . . .

LUISA: I'm sure you can fix things.

BERGMAN: Save his job, you mean?

LUISA: If that's what it comes to.

BERGMAN: Bergman the fixer. Sorting out, defending, explaining, manoeuvring. Not even any gratitude, they despise me for it! How I'd love to change places with that boy! To say any damned thing I like knowing there's always some ageing idiot to pull me out of it – wouldn't that be marvellous!

LUISA: You should be glad to have someone like him around.

BERGMAN: You're fond of him, aren't you?

LUISA: At least he's a real person.

BERGMAN: Unlike me? . . . Good-looking too.

LUISA: Yes, that too.

BERGMAN: Yes. Well, it's understandable for a woman of your age to want to dispense her bounty in that direction.

LUISA: And I suppose it's understandable for a man of your age to see everything in the crudest terms.

(*Pause.*)

How are you feeling?

BERGMAN: In one sense, better.

LUISA: In what sense?

BERGMAN: I went up to the tower this morning.

LUISA: What for? Meditation?

BERGMAN: Yes. With that legend of Plekhanov's in my mind. I stood there for ages looking down at the moat . . .

LUISA: And did you find enlightenment?

BERGMAN: Oh yes. I realized that it would be quick and easy. And very possible . . .

(*The* SPECIAL SECRETARY *enters by the right upper door, crosses the gallery quickly, runs down to the left door and goes out. Slight pause.*)

LUISA: Will you speak to him about those men?

BERGMAN: What men?

LUISA: Those two in the dungeon.

BERGMAN: I will at the right moment. He's obviously taken up with something just now.
(*Pause.*)
You're not interested.

LUISA: In what?

BERGMAN: I was talking about the tower.

LUISA: Oh, that. You know, I've been thinking over what you said yesterday . . .

BERGMAN: And what conclusion did you reach?

LUISA: That it *is* more complicated than I thought . . .

BERGMAN: Ah!

LUISA: I don't know about its being metaphysical, but it's certainly not just psychological. I'd call it existential. Here you are, playing the role of the wise man guarding our studio from the turmoil of the world, and not making a bad job of it; at the same time, deep inside, you suspect that this role is nothing but fancy dress, behind which hides a rather ordinary conformist thrashing about in a rather ordinary way. And of course this doubt about the reality of your role includes a doubt about your own identity, even your very existence: if your grand mission is merely an illusion, the terrifying thought must have struck you that the illusion extends to your very self.
(*The* SPECIAL SECRETARY *enters by the right rear door, hurries across the room, runs up the staircase and out by the left upper door.*)
Such thoughts must be hard to live with. So you look for a way out, a way to convince yourself that you actually exist as a real person. It's not to be found in your public life, so you look to the private one. In other words, you use your anxieties, depressions, death wishes, to demonstrate at every moment that you are a man and not a fiction; your obsession with non-existence proves your existence, your preoccupation with death proves you're still alive . . .
(*The* SPECIAL SECRETARY *enters by the left door and runs down towards the right rear door.*)

BERGMAN: Is something going on?

SPECIAL SECRETARY: Not for the moment . . .

(*He goes out by the right rear door.*)

LUISA: The trouble is of course that it's all a fake, all a substitute. Your posturings about private pressures cover your lack of public courage. So in fact you commit a further fraud on yourself, escaping from one illusion into another, robbing Peter to pay Paul. Sooner or later you'll realize this, see that you're nothing but illusions, substitutions and borrowings, that there are no more Peters to rob. Only *then* will you be seized by a real despair and a real wish to die. And only then will I seriously begin to fear for you . . .

(*Slight pause. Then* BERGMAN *suddenly begins to sob like a child. For a moment* LUISA *looks at him in surprise; then she goes up to him and begins gently to kiss the tears from his eyes.*) There there . . . No, stop it, I didn't mean to hurt you . . . I was only trying to help . . .

(*The* SPECIAL SECRETARY *enters by the left rear door.* LUISA *draws away from* BERGMAN, *who tries to return to normal.*)

SPECIAL SECRETARY: Are all your people in the building?

BERGMAN: Yes. Why?

SPECIAL SECRETARY: Call them together, please, at once.

BERGMAN: Is something going on?

SPECIAL SECRETARY: You'll see soon enough.

(*He goes out by the right door, leaving it open as he goes.*
BERGMAN *goes to the stairs and calls out towards the left door.*)

BERGMAN: Renata!

LUISA: Wipe your eyes.

(RENATA *enters by the left door and stands on the landing.*)

BERGMAN: Call everybody, will you?

RENATA: Now?

BERGMAN: Yes, now!

(RENATA *runs downstairs towards the left rear door as* ULCH *enters on to the gallery from the right upper door.*)

ULCH: Renata, I must talk to you!

RENATA: There's no time now, we have a meeting.

ULCH: After the meeting then . . .

(*But* RENATA *has gone out by the left rear door.* ULCH *comes downstairs slowly.* ALBERT *enters by the left rear door,*

166

followed by RENATA, *who makes straight for the right rear door and out. A dog begins to bark wildly outside; everybody stops and looks towards the right door.* RENATA *comes in through the right rear door, followed by* PLEKHANOV *carrying his violin, which he deposits carefully, looking towards the right door, as does* RENATA. *The barking stops. A slight pause, as they wait in suspense.*)

SPECIAL SECRETARY: (*Offstage*) Hallo!

FIRST INSPECTOR: (*Offstage*) *Ciao!* Are they ready for me, Mishak?

SPECIAL SECRETARY: (*Offstage*) All ready.

(MACOURKOVA *runs in panting by the left rear door. After a slight pause the* FIRST INSPECTOR *enters by the right door. He is black. The* SPECIAL SECRETARY *follows him, closing the door after him. They stop on the stairs. The others watch, confused, but the* FIRST INSPECTOR *gazes round with a smile.*)

FIRST INSPECTOR: *Ciao!*

BERGMAN: (*Uncertainly*) *Ciao* . . .

SPECIAL SECRETARY: It's my pleasant duty to introduce our new Inspector of Projects, his predecessor having gone into well-deserved retirement. Our friend here wishes to say a few words about his views on the project . . .

FIRST INSPECTOR: Sit down, please, make yourselves comfortable.

(*Bewildered, they all sit down round the table. The* FIRST INSPECTOR *sits on the stairs by the right door, the* SPECIAL SECRETARY *sitting next to him.*)

Right, now, you're all expecting a long boring speech. Well, you're not getting one. We've all had our bellyful of bullshit, right?

(*Nervous laughter.*)

That's the first thing. Second: let's not be *afraid* of each other. We're all in the same boat, right? Which at the moment is paddling backwards up shit creek, right?

(*Nervous laughter.* PLEKHANOV *in particular gives an incredulous laugh, twanging his fiddle.*)

MACOURKOVA: Excuse me, Inspector –

FIRST INSPECTOR: Miss –

MACOURKOVA: Macourkova, Mrs Macourkova. I wondered if
you'd care for a cup of coffee?

FIRST INSPECTOR: No offence, Mrs M., but I had a cup of the
real thing this morning, special issue, know what I mean?
(*Polite laughter*.)
Now, I may be the new boy, right, but I'm not stupid. I
sussed out this situation p.d. bloody q. Some thickhead at
the top tells you what to do, right? And you say, yes sir, no
sir, three bags full, sir. Get out of order and you're im
shtook, am I right?
(*They nod in bewilderment*.)
Friends, those days are over. Put it this way, you're ace
architects, you don't want a bunch of know-nothing
dickheads talking out of their arses at you from Mount
Olympus, pardon my Polish. Let's face it, this whole
project was a pig's ear from day one, you know it, I know
it, even they know it down there. Now don't get me wrong;
better pads with plumbing, sewerage, and all mod. cons,
no one's arguing. But bulldozing the lot and shoving up
highrises? Forget it. That's the simple way, yes, so was
Dresden. But it offends your susceptibilities because it's
bloody outrageous, am I right?
(*They nod in bewilderment*.)
What they don't dig up there is that people are individuals,
they want to do their own thing, know what I mean?
Here's a pigeon-fancier, there's a rabbit-man, why not if
that's their bag? This was my manor, friends, I was
dragged up here so I know what I'm talking about. But to
get to the nitty-gritty: bulldozing is out, right. So what's
in, you ask? How the fuck should we know, excuse my
Estonian? You're the experts, you tell us, it's your ball-
game. Use your expertise, focus those fine-tuned brains on
the problem and come up with something fantastic! Not for
here, maybe, don't feel tied down, if you get some fab
notion that won't work here, it might work somewhere else
and we can do a swap. Know what I mean?
(*A short embarrassed pause*.)

BERGMAN: I think I speak not only for myself but for all my colleagues when I –

FIRST INSPECTOR: You are – excuse me?

BERGMAN: Zdenek Bergman. I'm the Project Director.

FIRST INSPECTOR: So you're in charge here?

BERGMAN: Only if you want me to be, I mean . . .

FIRST INSPECTOR: It's not what I want, friend. They're the ones! (*To the others*) You reckon this fella?

(*They nod.*)

Fair enough, you got the job. Only cut the crap, keep it short, know what I mean?

BERGMAN: Yes. I think I speak for all of us in saying that we've waited years for this moment. By its nature, you see, architecture desperately needs freedom –

FIRST INSPECTOR: Well, there you go! You're on your own. Any hassle, just give me a bell. Better still, tell Mishak here, *he*'ll give me a bell. What are Special Secretaries for? So –

(*The* FIRST INSPECTOR *gets up, followed by the* SPECIAL SECRETARY *and then everyone else.*)

So good luck! Good luck!

ALBERT: Inspector . . .

FIRST INSPECTOR: Uhuh?

ALBERT: I don't know whether you know, but some time ago when we were still at the planning stage, two of the townspeople brought up a petition criticizing the scheme. The result was that they were interned in the dungeon. Couldn't this injustice be put right?

FIRST INSPECTOR: Let them out, Mishak!

SPECIAL SECRETARY: Both of them?

FIRST INSPECTOR: Both of them, yes! So, friends – *Ciao!*

ALL: *Ciao!*

(*The* FIRST INSPECTOR *waves and leaves, by the right door, with the* SPECIAL SECRETARY. *A stunned silence as they all stare at the right door.*)

ALBERT: Freedom!

(*The others come to themselves; saying 'Freedom', embracing each other.*)

PLEKHANOV: I've seen some changes in my time, but I never dreamed the likes of this. Did you, Zdenek?

BERGMAN: Oh, I dreamed it . . .

LUISA: Maybe it *is* a dream.

ALBERT: No! *That* was the dream! It had to happen – we've woken up! We're alive again!

PLEKHANOV: For as long as it lasts . . .

BERGMAN: It's got to last!

ALBERT: No more excuses for us now!

BERGMAN: Once in a lifetime! It's got to last!

(*They subside slowly; some of them sit at the table.* RENATA *stands to one side. Slight pause.*)

ULCH: I don't wish to be a wet blanket . . .

LUISA: Ulch, you're not going to carp at this as well.

ULCH: No, of course I'm delighted. I'm only afraid we may be in danger of throwing the baby out with the bathwater . . .

BERGMAN: What are you talking about, Ulch?

ULCH: I only want to point out that to break free from incompetent management is one thing; to throw overboard all rational thinking on town planning is something else . . .

LUISA: Who's talking about throwing anything overboard?

ULCH: Nobody yet; but I foresee moves in that direction. Personally, I have to make my position clear: I refuse to subscribe to any attempt to take urban architectonics back to the primitive, chaotic and antisocial forms of the last century –

BERGMAN: None of us wants that, Ulch! You're crying doom unnecessarily, my friend.

ULCH: Maybe so, but the point had to be made. As I see it, it's essential that our dislike of centralism doesn't degenerate into a dislike of conceptualization in general . . .

PLEKHANOV: You talk as if there are only two possibilities: bureaucratic control or anarchy –

ALBERT: Exactly! To promote pluralism instead of uniformism isn't to choose chaos instead of order but life instead of death!

170

ULCH: I've nothing against pluralism! Just to remind you that freedom doesn't mean irresponsibility!

BERGMAN: Absolutely! As I see it, freedom means not irresponsibility but a golden chance to finally fulfil our creative responsibility! It's primarily a moral question: we must put truth above lies, courage above conformity, freedom above repression. The braver we are as people, the better we'll be as architects. Let's be honest: we've spent years designing bad buildings. Why? I'll tell you: because we were never given our heads! Of course some of us will think globally, others individualistically. The main thing is that we do what we want to do, not what we are forced to do. Our projects must be born in an atmosphere of free discussion, mutual tolerance, Ulch, good will and efficient collaboration. To create and defend such an atmosphere is the task we must now set ourselves.

PLEKHANOV: No more taboos.

ALBERT: Fear must give way to truth!

BERGMAN: Obedience must give way to responsibility!

LUISA: Stupidity must give way to freedom!

BERGMAN: What is your opinion about all this, Mrs Macourkova?

(MACOURKOVA *shrugs her shoulders indecisively.*)

MACOURKOVA: Oh well, you know . . .

(*Slight pause.*)

BERGMAN: Yes . . .

LUISA: Is this a good time for the celebration bubbly?

BERGMAN: What better?

(LUISA *gestures to* RENATA, *and they go out by the left rear door. As they do so, the* SPECIAL SECRETARY *comes through the right rear door, with the* TWO DELEGATES.)

PLEKHANOV: 'And the graves shall open . . .'

BERGMAN: Welcome to freedom, my friend. Didn't I tell you not to worry? And have no fears about your town, we shan't ruin it.

FIRST DELEGATE: Thank you.

BERGMAN: No no, the thanks are ours. We see now that we

have a common cause; we fight together. Our greetings to
the town! *Ciao!*

FIRST DELEGATE: *Ciao.*

SECOND DELEGATE: *Ciao.*

(*They go towards the right door with the* SPECIAL
SECRETARY.)

MACOURKOVA: Secretary . . .

SPECIAL SECRETARY: Yes?

MACOURKOVA: Won't you stay for a little drink with us? We're
celebrating.

SPECIAL SECRETARY: I never drink. *Ciao* . . .

MACOURKOVA: *Ciao.*

(*The* SPECIAL SECRETARY *goes out by the right door, as*
LUISA *and* RENATA *enter by the left rear door*, LUISA *with a
tray of glasses*, RENATA *with four bottles of champagne*. LUISA
passes out the glasses, BERGMAN *and* PLEKHANOV *take two of
the bottles, while* RENATA *puts the other two on the table*.
BERGMAN *and* PLEKHANOV *open the bottles with a pop and
fill the glasses*.)

RENATA: Real champagne!

LUISA: Or almost!

BERGMAN: (*Raising his glass*) Colleagues! I give you a toast! To
the unfettered advance of architecture! To urbanism with a
human face!

ALL: (*Clinking glasses*) Urbanism with a human face!

(*They drink*. BERGMAN *and* PLEKHANOV *refill their glasses*.)

PLEKHANOV: (*Raising his glass*) I drink to the end of official
vandalism!

ALL: (*Clinking glasses*) Hurray!

LUISA: (*Raising her glass*) I drink to the death of fear!

ALL: (*Clinking glasses*) Hurray!

PLEKHANOV: *Now* I can play a jolly tune!

(*He seizes his fiddle and begins to play the 'Blue Danube'
waltz*.)

LUISA: And now we can dance!

(BERGMAN *takes* LUISA, *and begins to dance*.)

BERGMAN: Why aren't you dancing? You are all to dance!
That's an order!

ALBERT: No more orders!

ULCH: Down with orders! But everyone must dance!

(ULCH *grabs* RENATA, ALBERT *takes* MACOURKOVA *and they begin to dance. After a while they change partners:* BERGMAN *dances with* MACOURKOVA, ULCH *with* LUISA, ALBERT *with* RENATA. PLEKHANOV *speeds up the tempo, they grow wilder in their dancing. After a while the men again change partners:* BERGMAN *is now with* RENATA, ULCH *with* MACOURKOVA, ALBERT *with* LUISA. PLEKHANOV *speeds up still more, the dance grows still wilder and more elaborate. This goes on for some time, till the dancers are becoming visibly exhausted and rather unsteady with the champagne; they return gradually to the table and sit down, out of breath.* PLEKHANOV *stops playing, puts down his fiddle. A slight pause. Then* LUISA *grabs the other two bottles and gives them to* PLEKHANOV *and* BERGMAN, *who open them and pour more champagne.*)

ALBERT: Architects of the world, unite!

(*Hubbub.*)

ULCH: Special Secretaries of the world, depart for the next world!

(*Hubbub. They drain their glasses.* BERGMAN *and* PLEKHANOV *repour.*)

LUISA: Citizens of the world, love everybody in the world!

(*Hubbub.* PLEKHANOV *again seizes his fiddle and begins to play a wild csárdás.* LUISA *jumps on the table and begins to dance.* ULCH *collapses on the ground.* MACOURKOVA *takes him by the feet and, staggering, drags him towards the left rear door and out.* BERGMAN *gets up meanwhile, grabs the bottle and pours the rest of its contents over his head, after which he staggers to the staircase, falls against it and collapses to the floor.* RENATA, *who has drunk least, runs to him and eventually manages to get him to his feet, his arm round her neck, and helps him upstairs and goes out with him by the left door.* LUISA *continues to dance on the table, more wildly and provocatively, while* ALBERT *sits gazing up at her. There is a dissonant screech on the fiddle and* PLEKHANOV *stops playing, lets the fiddle fall from his hands, lets his head sink to his chest and immediately falls into a snoring sleep.* LUISA *stops dancing, laughs, sits on the table near* ALBERT *and turns to him.*)

ALBERT: You're wonderful . . .

(LUISA *begins to laugh. She takes the polystyrene model of the town with its castle, puts it on her head like an extraordinary hat, crosses her legs provocatively and assumes the pose of a courtesan.* ALBERT, *ignoring this, takes her hand and begins to speak rapidly, ignoring* PLEKHANOV's *snoring, which will accompany his whole speech.*)

Luisa — I know you'll probably make fun of me, but I'm absolutely serious about this: I love you! I love you madly. Of course it's ridiculous, it's stupid and mad. I know it's hopeless. I don't want anything from you, I've forbidden myself to want anything. It's entirely my problem, I've no right to bother you with it . . . It's enough for me just to see you now and then, during a meeting or at dinner . . . I respect your relationship with the chief, I'd give up my job rather than cause you the slightest trouble . . . This is the first and last time I shall mention it, I promise . . . Nothing like this has ever happened to me before . . . I don't understand it, I curse myself for it . . . but it's too strong for me . . . I probably wouldn't ever have mentioned it if it weren't for that wretched champagne . . . You're the sun in my life, all I want is the occasional ray falling on me from afar . . . that's all I need . . . I never dreamed love was like this, like falling over a precipice without the slightest control . . . My heart starts pounding whenever I see you, I'm behaving like a schoolboy, talking like a schoolboy . . . can't you help, make it stop, stamp on it, laugh at it, tell the chief, make it a house joke . . . I can't work, I see you all the time, everywhere, I've done no work for days now . . . Every night I have agonizing dreams about you . . . I hate myself that I can't control it, can't make it stop . . . I used to think I was a man, I was proud of my strong will, my self-control, suddenly I'm overwhelmed with feelings I don't understand . . . Not feelings, something else, something outside me, a demon possessing me . . . You're the one centre of my universe,

my axis, the source of my reality and meaning . . . I don't
understand why God is testing me like this . . .
(*During* ALBERT's *speech* LUISA *grows serious; she slowly
removes her 'hat', tears come to her eyes, and she finally bursts
into a loud sobbing.* ALBERT *stops.* LUISA *sits on the table,
curled up in a ball, her hands covering her face.* ALBERT,
confused, gets up, not knowing what to do. Then he approaches
LUISA *cautiously and gently strokes her hair. She turns to him,
still crying, pulls him to her and kisses him. Then she gently
pushes him away. She controls her crying, dries her eyes, and
tries to smile.*)

LUISA: I'm sorry. We're both idiots . . . drunken idiots . . .
ALBERT: Have I hurt you?
LUISA: Oh no . . .
ALBERT: Why are you crying?
LUISA: You wouldn't understand . . .
ALBERT: Please tell me.
LUISA: For myself.
(*She smiles sadly at him, then goes up to him and embraces
him, and begins to kiss him gently.* ALBERT's *eyes are closed;
he stands there stupefied.* RENATA *enters by the left door.
Seeing* LUISA *and* ALBERT *embracing, she stares at them in
horror.* LUISA *gives* ALBERT *a final kiss and steps away from
him, looking at him with a smile.* ALBERT's *eyes remain
closed.*)
(*Softly*) Albert . . .
(ALBERT *opens his eyes.*)
Enough now . . . I must be a sensible little girl. And you
must be a sensible little boy. Promise me you'll be a
sensible little boy?
(ALBERT *nods slightly.* RENATA *begins to sob quietly. Then the
left rear door flies open and* ULCH *hurtles on, wearing only a
shirt and underpants. His trousers and lab. coat come flying in
after him.* ULCH *stops, looks round, sees* RENATA.)
ULCH: I have a sex drive too!
RENATA: (*Overcoming her sobbing*) I know you do . . .
(PLEKHANOV *suddenly wakes up with a start, obviously from*

*some kind of awful dream. He looks ahead in alarm for a
moment, then realizes where he is, picks up his fiddle and
begins to play again the 'Blue Danube' waltz. As the lights dim
the music grows fainter till it cannot be heard.)*

ACT IV

The fiddle is heard playing 'Ochi Cherniya'. As the lights go up
PLEKHANOV *is seen playing, a white handkerchief round his head*
like a bandage. ALBERT *sits disconsolately nearby. A pause.*
RENATA *enters by the left door and stops on the landing, unnoticed*
by the other two.

RENATA: Excuse me, sir . . .
    (*Not hearing,* PLEKHANOV *plays on. A pause.*)
    Mr Plekhanov, sir . . .
    (*Still no response.*)
    Excuse me, sir!
    (PLEKHANOV *stops playing.*)
PLEKHANOV: Are you talking to me?
RENATA: The Project Director wondered if you had any more of
    your pills . . .
PLEKHANOV: My apologies, but I gave the last one to friend
    Ulch just now.
RENATA: I'll give him the message.
    (*She exits by the left door.* PLEKHANOV *puts down his fiddle.*)
PLEKHANOV: Albert, you really ought to have a little talk with
    Renata. Can't you see she's eating her heart out?
ALBERT: Over me?
PLEKHANOV: My head's splitting . . .
ALBERT: So's mine . . .
PLEKHANOV: I realize you have other things on your mind. I
    went through it myself twenty years ago. Even so . . .
ALBERT: I don't know what you went through twenty years ago,
    and you don't know what I'm going through now.
PLEKHANOV: But I do. We were at college together, I was in
    just the same boat as you are. Only of course she was
    twenty years younger then . . .
ALBERT: Are you talking about – ?
PLEKHANOV: Of course I am.
ALBERT: Has she told you anything?

177

PLEKHANOV: What about?

ALBERT: What happened yesterday.

PLEKHANOV: I don't know anything about yesterday; but I know what's going on with you.

ALBERT: Whatever you think you know, you don't understand.

PLEKHANOV: On the contrary, I'm the only one who does understand. I look at you and I see my younger self. That's why I'm worried about you.

ALBERT: Why?

PLEKHANOV: You don't know what you're getting into. I'm not in the habit of meddling with other people's affairs, but in this case . . .

ALBERT: Go on if you must.

PLEKHANOV: Your love appeals to her, you see, Albert, attracts her, excites her, that's why she can't put a stop to it. But at the same time she's incapable of taking that last wild step which would bring it to a head and save you. So she'll keep your love alive without ever fulfilling it. Sooner or later it'll drive you out of your mind, and there'll come some sort of casual tragedy. Believe me, I know what I'm talking about.

ALBERT: It happened to you? I mean . . .

PLEKHANOV: Never mind me, you're the one we're concerned with. Kill it, Albert, kill it now inside you, or you never will, unless you kill yourself, which I hope is not in your mind. After a certain stage, you know, some illnesses are incurable . . .

ALBERT: Love isn't an illness! Not love for her . . . Or do you think she's – a bad person?

PLEKHANOV: Bad? Not at all! That's the problem! That game she plays, you know, vague promises and partial repulses, those provocative hints at a longing, always in the end triumphantly controlled, that mixture of intimacy and inaccessibility – if that were just cold-blooded calculation or frivolous irresponsibility you'd see through it and cope with it. No, the devil of it is that she destroys not out of malice or simple-mindedness but out of her very nature . . . I apologize for the sermon. Put it down to that inner voice you talked about not so long ago.

(*Pause.*)

ALBERT: It's odd.

PLEKHANOV: What is?

ALBERT: You try to warn me off her, and you've done the opposite: I'm beginning to understand that special sadness I see in her eyes . . .

PLEKHANOV: And that makes you feel even closer to her.

ALBERT: Yes.

PLEKHANOV: It intensifies your longing to help her.

ALBERT: Yes.

PLEKHANOV: You see that in this unfeeling world only your selfless love can protect her from the unhappiness she unconsciously creates for herself by unconsciously creating it in others . . .

ALBERT: Yes, yes.

PLEKHANOV: I was afraid that might happen. So I'd best do what I should have done in the first place: wish you good luck and hold my tongue.

(RENATA *enters by the left door with two cups of coffee on a tray, and goes slowly upstairs.* PLEKHANOV *nudges* ALBERT *to speak to her.*)

ALBERT: Renata . . .

(*She stops, then speaks without turning.*)

RENATA: Yes?

ALBERT: Do you have a few moments?

RENATA: I'm sorry but –

ALBERT: It's important.

RENATA: I have work to do.

ALBERT: We all have work to do. Please . . .

RENATA: I really can't just now . . .

(*She goes out quickly by the left upper door.* ALBERT *looks at* PLEKHANOV.)

PLEKHANOV: She's embarrassed. Run after her.

(*He gives* ALBERT *a little push, and* ALBERT *begins to go upstairs. But when he is only about three stairs up the left door opens and* LUISA *enters, a cup of coffee in each hand, leaving the*

179

door open. ALBERT *goes down, flustered, to make way for her.*)

ALBERT: (*Quietly*) Good morning . . .

LUISA: (*Cheerfully*) Good morning, Albert.

> (*She takes her cups to the table.* PLEKHANOV *picks up his fiddle. Seeing him, the handkerchief round his head, she laughs.*)

You're not looking your usual self, Kuzma. Not like the Kuzma of old.

PLEKHANOV: (*Scowling*) I think I shall have a lie down . . .

> (*He shuffles out by the right rear door.* LUISA *puts the coffee down, one for her, one for* BERGMAN, *sits and begins to stir hers; she glances at* ALBERT, *who still stands uneasily on the stairs. She smiles at him. A pause.*)

ALBERT: (*Quietly*) Forgive me . . .

LUISA: What for?

ALBERT: What happened yesterday.

LUISA: Don't be an idiot . . .

> (BERGMAN *enters by the left door, his head also bandaged with a handkerchief.*)

ALBERT: Good morning.

> (BERGMAN *gives a curt nod and goes to his place at the table. Forgetting that he was to go after* RENATA, ALBERT *wanders about indecisively for a moment or two, then:*)

I think I'll have a lie down too . . .

> (*And he goes out by the left rear door.* BERGMAN, *sitting at his place, stirs his coffee. A pause.*)

BERGMAN: So how are you coping with the new – development?

LUISA: You can't expect me not to be touched.

BERGMAN: Touched, of course: love begets love.

LUISA: I said nothing about love.

BERGMAN: I'm sorry, let it remain unspoken . . . But you don't want to leave it there, surely?

LUISA: Maybe not, but I shall.

BERGMAN: Why is that?

LUISA: You wouldn't understand.

BERGMAN: No, of course I'm a man of stone as everyone knows. Feelings are your territory.

LUISA: It's your cynicism makes them my territory.

BERGMAN: Why will you leave it there?

LUISA: Because it's too serious to play with. I have no right. In case you haven't noticed, my territory includes responsibility from time to time.

BERGMAN: I'm afraid my brain is too coarse to figure out what can be so terribly serious about a sensitive and apparently innocent young man getting his head turned by an experienced woman in her forties. Still, I can be flattered: I suppose his falling for you is a kind of back-handed tribute to my good taste . . .

LUISA: Oh, he's only doing it to flatter you. Look, do you think we could try to be serious for a moment?

BERGMAN: I'm all for experiment.

LUISA: In the first place, I'd rather you didn't blame me for everything. I didn't set out to turn his head, I was as surprised as you were. Secondly, this is not a casual lust of the kind we're used to around here. There are depths we've forgotten about, if we ever knew them, and they're dangerous.

BERGMAN: For him, you mean?

LUISA: Perhaps for me too.

BERGMAN: One looks into the depths and wishes to fall . . .

LUISA: Well put.

BERGMAN: And is filled with terror.

LUISA: Quite so.

BERGMAN: So in fact you're afraid! You've looked into the depths . . .

LUISA: A glimpse.

BERGMAN: Not in my bed, I trust.

LUISA: If you're going to be tasteless we won't discuss it!

BERGMAN: Sorry. So how did you peer in?

LUISA: He told me terrifying things. Beautiful, but terrifying.

BERGMAN: For instance?

LUISA: That I'm the sun in his life, that he wants nothing more than for one of my rays to fall upon him from afar . . .

BERGMAN: What else?

LUISA: That his heart starts to pound the moment he sees me . . .

BERGMAN: Go on.

LUISA: He feels as if he's possessed by a demon. I'm the hub of his universe, the only source of its reality and meaning.

(*The* SPECIAL SECRETARY *enters by the left door. He goes quickly upstairs, across the gallery and out through the right upper door.*)

BERGMAN: How strange.

LUISA: What is?

BERGMAN: That you, that well-known critic of the banal, should suddenly start to enjoy it.

LUISA: If you knew the smallest thing about love you'd know that the deeper the feeling, the harder it is to talk about; at its deepest, triteness is often all that works.

BERGMAN: I'll take your word for it. To get back to your famous sense of responsibility, does responsibility for me play any part in your considerations?

LUISA: Would you be upset if it didn't?

BERGMAN: I'm only interested.

LUISA: And I'm interested to know if you'd be upset.

BERGMAN: You needn't concern yourself with that any longer.

LUISA: What's that supposed to mean?

BERGMAN: Only that whatever happens I can't feel worse than I do now.

(*The* SPECIAL SECRETARY *enters by the right rear door and heads for the stairs.*)

Is anything wrong?

SPECIAL SECRETARY: Not at the moment.

(*He goes quickly upstairs and out by the left upper door.*)

LUISA: So here we go again.

BERGMAN: What do you mean?

LUISA: Turning the conversation back to your favourite subject. You're like a totally predictable character in a totally predictable play. Only since the last time I fell for your performance I've made a decision: not to buy another ticket. You can't put on your drama without an audience, can you? I wonder I didn't think of it long ago. I'm obviously one of those people who don't know what a play's about until they've seen it fifty times – Where are you going?

(BERGMAN *has stood up and is walking towards the stairs and up. He stops on the landing.*)

BERGMAN: Some plays, Luisa, you'll never understand until they're taken out of the repertory. As this one; you'll see. The performance is over, my love. Only this time the audience won't walk out of the play; the play will walk out of the audience. I hope you've enjoyed it . . .

(*He turns and slowly, even ceremoniously, continues up the stairs.* LUISA *watches for a moment without understanding; then she jumps to her feet.*)

LUISA: Zdenek!

BERGMAN: What do you want?

LUISA: Where the hell are you going?

BERGMAN: To the tower . . .

(*He is already on the gallery and on his way to the right upper door.* LUISA *runs up after him.*)

LUISA: Have you gone mad? Wait!

(*She catches up with him and blocks his way.* BERGMAN *pushes her away, but she grabs him and holds on tight. He tries to shake her off. There is a scuffle.*)

BERGMAN: Let go of me!

LUISA: Do you want me to make a scene? I'm going to scream . . .

BERGMAN: Do as you like. This is the end. Don't you understand? The end of everything! Will you let me go! (*The noise has attracted the others.* ULCH *appears at the right upper door, a handkerchief round his head;* RENATA *at the left door;* ALBERT *at the left rear door; and at the right rear door,* PLEKHANOV *with his fiddle, his head still bound.*)

ULCH: I have a headache! What's going on?

LUISA: Stop him! Hang on to him!

(*In front of the right upper door* ULCH *struggles with* BERGMAN, *who is trying to escape; with their bound heads they struggle like Japanese wrestlers.* PLEKHANOV *puts down his fiddle and runs up to the gallery, followed by* ALBERT.)

BERGMAN: Ulch, I order you to let me go!

PLEKHANOV: What are we stopping him from doing?

LUISA: Don't ask questions, just stop him!

(PLEKHANOV, ULCH *and* ALBERT *hold on to* BERGMAN
firmly. BERGMAN *struggles for a while, then gives up.*)

BERGMAN: All right! Enough! I'll come.

(PLEKHANOV, ULCH *and* ALBERT *cautiously let him go.*
BERGMAN *goes slowly back along the gallery; as he passes*
LUISA *he hisses*:)

I'll still do it!

(*Just before* BERGMAN *reaches the left upper door the* SPECIAL
SECRETARY *comes out of it at speed and, taking no notice of*
anyone, dashes downstairs, crosses the hall and out by the right
door, which he leaves open. BERGMAN, *the others following,*
comes quietly down the stairs. There is a pause as everyone
stands anxiously around the table.)

PLEKHANOV: What's come over you, chief, for God's sake? And
now of all times, just when things are finally changing for
the better . . .

ULCH: Alcohol poisoning. Some people are worse with a
hangover than when they're drunk.

ALBERT: It's all my fault . . .

PLEKHANOV: Nonsense!

ALBERT: I know it is, don't try and comfort me.

LUISA: Oh, don't be an idiot.

(BERGMAN, *aware that everyone is staring at him, looks round*
at them meaningfully. Slight pause.)

BERGMAN: I'm not going to explain myself; you wouldn't
understand anyway. It's nothing to do with the project, still
less to do with you, Albert. If you must have a reason,
alcohol poisoning will do. But I'd prefer it if you'd forget
the whole sorry episode . . .

(*A dog starts barking wildly outside. Everyone looks curiously*
towards the right door. The barking stops. MACOURKOVA, *out*
of breath, runs in by the left rear door. Soon afterwards, the
SECOND INSPECTOR *enters by the right door, followed by the*
SPECIAL SECRETARY, *who closes the door behind him.*
BERGMAN, PLEKHANOV *and* ULCH *take off their*
handkerchiefs and put them in their pockets. As everyone
watches them anxiously, the SECOND INSPECTOR *and the*
SPECIAL SECRETARY *cross the stage pompously and climb the*

184

stairs, stopping in the middle of the gallery. The SECOND
INSPECTOR *takes a small sheet of paper from his pocket, clears
his throat and begins to read. The* SPECIAL SECRETARY *stands
just behind him, looking over his shoulder at the paper as he
reads.*)

SECOND INSPECTOR: (*Reading*) 'From time to time it becomes
necessary to bite on the apple no matter how sour; even,
sometimes, in the interests of the well-being of the people,
to take out the scalpel and excise the abscess. It hurts for a
while, but then the whole organism feels better. Some of
you may not find it easy at first to accept without question
or reservation what I am about to say. Finally, however,
you will reconcile yourselves to it, realizing that to use the
scalpel was the only way to save the patient.'

(MACOURKOVA *tiptoes out through the left rear door.*)

'My predecessor, whom you met here recently, was not a
bad fellow. Unfortunately, as you no doubt surmised
during your brief meeting, he fell short intellectually,
temperamentally and professionally of the demands of the
situation.'

(MACOURKOVA *returns by the left rear door with a glass of
water. She tiptoes across and up the stairs to put the glass on
the gallery railing in front of the* SECOND INSPECTOR, *then
goes quickly downstairs to join the others. The* SECOND
INSPECTOR *takes a drink and continues reading.*)

'A tragic figure, one could say: a simple man, a native of
this area, well intentioned and attuned to the mood of the
people but inexperienced in management, weak in public
relations and conceptually unsound. Thus it was that,
failing to sense the moment when freedom turns to
anarchy, unable in the hysterical atmosphere of unregulated
discussion to distinguish between those with honest ideas
and those without, he lost control of the situation. And so,
in his attempt to strengthen your autonomy as architects, to
listen to the voice of the people and so to improve the
quality of your work, he produced the direct opposite:
confusion spread and finally work here came to a complete
standstill . . .'

(*He pauses, looks down at the listeners and apparently begins to extemporize.*)

And if you don't work, what happens? I'll tell you, you don't eat! If you want to eat you've got to keep your nose to the grindstone! It's true for everyone! Even our grandmothers knew that. It's how things are! It's a fact of life! Anyone who doesn't understand that, what happens? He learns the hard way, through his teeth!

(*The* SPECIAL SECRETARY *gives the* SECOND INSPECTOR *an inconspicuous little nudge; the* SECOND INSPECTOR *understands at once and returns to the prepared text.*)

'Only after much urging from a number of honest people have I taken on the thankless task of restoring normality. But I shall not throw the baby out with the bathwater. On the contrary, I shall lift out the child, dry it off and nurse it to health that it may thrive and grow beautiful. But so that you don't think I'm a man of the old era, slavishly mouthing endless streams of meaningless verbiage, let me come straight to the point at issue: The decision to abandon the planned redevelopment project was rash, irresponsible, unprofessional and damaging, a stab to the heart of your mission, which is, to create better living conditions in a truly modern and conceptual manner. Preparations for the project will therefore continue as before, but with a new dynamism! Certain people will try to convince you that this is a return to old rightfully rejected methods. On the contrary! This is a radical renewal of the original intention, and a radical cleansing of former deformities calling for critical reform, as well as of all later excesses resulting from this criticism. I am confident that reason will triumph over emotion even among you, that even you will understand the urgent need for the necessary surgery, and that you will throw yourselves into the work with renewed vigour to make up for the unnecessary delay of the past weeks, which has caused such unease to the people down there. Good luck!'

(*He folds his piece of paper, puts it in his pocket, but feels it necessary to extemporize again.*)

Everyone's clamouring for a new toilet, tiles in the
bathroom, white's not enough these days, they want black
and God knows what! That's the way it is! That's the
reality. Only that means someone's got to do what? Install
it for them, yes! And before that, what? Design it, yes!
That's how it always was and always will be, it's a fact of
life, not just here, everywhere, anyone who doesn't
understand that will get their – !

(*The* SPECIAL SECRETARY *leans forward to whisper something
in his ear, pointing at his watch. The* SECOND INSPECTOR
nods, takes a drink of water, then together with the SPECIAL
SECRETARY *makes for the right door.*)

(*As he goes*) *Ciao* . . .

BERGMAN: *Ciao* . . .

(*The* SECOND INSPECTOR *and the* SPECIAL SECRETARY *go
out by the right door, leaving the others motionless, staring dully
after them. Long pause.*)

PLEKHANOV: So that's that.

(*He gives a little twang on his fiddle. A pause.*)

LUISA: We didn't enjoy that freedom for long.

(*A pause.*)

ULCH: I knew from the start it could only end one way. The last
man was obviously a rank amateur . . .

(*A pause.*)

LUISA: He wasn't too clever, I agree. But what would he be
doing in that job if he were?

(*A pause.*)

ULCH: You all laughed at me when I said we mustn't throw the
baby out with the bathwater. And now you see what's
happened.

(*A pause.*)

PLEKHANOV: Well, it was nice while it lasted.

LUISA: Like a dream.

PLEKHANOV: Better than a dream.

LUISA: At least we had a little dance.

PLEKHANOV: I just hope they're not tuning up for the big one.

LUISA: How is it we're so easily fooled?

PLEKHANOV: Only a corpse is never fooled.

(*After an embarrassed pause, they turn to look at* BERGMAN.)

BERGMAN: I think you're taking too gloomy a view, my friends. You know what I always say: what's done can't be undone, but every cloud has a silver lining. If you listened carefully you will have noticed that we're not required to revert *altogether* to the previous state of affairs. We've a little less room to manoeuvre, true, but we're used to that. We're going to have to bide our time for a while and keep our heads down. The first necessity in a new situation is to get one's proper bearings at the outset. We've lived through enough together – at least the older ones among us – to have the sense and experience to see this through as well. Personally I've never put much faith in great passions; easy come, easy go, I say. Less ambitious, more firmly based progress is of more value than high-flying manifestos. Manifestos don't build houses. We have to make careful assessments of what is practically feasible and what must be left temporarily in abeyance. We tried to run before we could walk, my friends, we made a number of high-sounding pronouncements with flowery words, forgetting that words are cheap. I include myself. One should not commit oneself to anything one is uncertain of being able to achieve. Feet on the ground, heads out of the clouds, we must cultivate the art of the possible. After all, architectural endeavour is never completely free, it exists in the social, economic and political context of the society it serves, a context it must respect. I'm not saying we shouldn't be bold. There are matters on which we must take a stance, points we must argue, that goes without question. All architects in all ages have had to decide when they should or must give way, and when they should stand firm. What is your opinion, Mrs Macourkova?

MACOURKOVA: Oh well, you know . . .

(*She shrugs her shoulders uncertainly.* ALBERT, *who has been listening carefully, suddenly speaks.*)

ALBERT: I'm getting out!

BERGMAN: I'm sorry?

ALBERT: I want to leave! This is making me sick!

BERGMAN: What is?

ALBERT: I don't understand what's going on! I don't understand anything.

BERGMAN: I can see this must have come as a shock to you, Albert, but a word of advice. Don't make rash decisions in the heat of the moment.

ALBERT: Do you remember yesterday? You were all trying to outdo each other! Never again would you betray your beliefs! Truth must destroy fear! Freedom must prevail over stupidity! And so on and so on, and then, suddenly, it's as if someone's waved a magic wand and you've been wiped clean, there's nothing left but how not to wet your pants as you run for cover! Is this normal? Does it go on everywhere? Are people just jellyfish? Am I mad, or are you?

(LUISA *goes up to* ALBERT *and pats him reassuringly*.)

LUISA: I understand your feelings, Albert, I really do. But try to understand us too. We shall need you now, more than ever. So promise me you'll be sensible.

ALBERT: I can't promise that, I'm sorry.

BERGMAN: As for those promises we made ourselves, Albert, they still stand. We simply have to find other ways of carrying them out. The fact is, in the excitement of the moment we let the idea of freedom go to our heads, unsurprisingly, and said some rather foolish things –

ALBERT: I didn't! I stand by everything I said!

BERGMAN: Albert, you're over-reacting. Calm down or you'll begin to make yourself ridiculous.

ALBERT: I don't care. I'd rather be ridiculous than lose my self-respect!

BERGMAN: I see. It's holier-than-thou you've decided to play, is it? The only one with clean hands? Well, please yourself. But I'm warning you, don't expect me to help next time you get yourself in a fix. If you want to put your head in a noose, go ahead and do it. But you're not going to put us in danger!

PLEKHANOV: Come, Zdenek, he's not putting us in danger.

BERGMAN: You know what he's trying to do? Prove himself a

real man! Well, as he knows himself, he's got a long way to
go!

ALBERT: What do you mean by that?

BERGMAN: I don't know what kind of real man it is whose heart
begins to pound every time he lays eyes on a sexually
inviting middle-aged woman.

LUISA: (*Shrieks*) Bergman!

BERGMAN: I won't take lessons in self-respect from a retarded
adolescent for whom a woman is the sun without whose
rays he cannot live, nay verily the hub of his universe!

LUISA: You're revolting!

(LUISA *puts her head in her hands and bursts into tears.*
ALBERT *looks despairingly at her, then at* BERGMAN, *then
back at* LUISA. *He stands helplessly for a moment like a beaten
dog, then suddenly runs upstairs as the* SPECIAL SECRETARY
*enters by the left upper door and blocks his way. For a moment
they look at each other silently.*)

SPECIAL SECRETARY: And where do you think you're going?
(*A slight pause.*)
Well? Struck dumb? You had enough to say a moment ago;
when you might have done well to listen to those wiser than
you . . .
(ALBERT *pushes the* SPECIAL SECRETARY *aside and tries to
pass him on the gallery. The* SPECIAL SECRETARY *seizes him
expertly by the hand and twists it;* ALBERT *writhes in agony.*)
What do you say now? Are you going to be a sensible little
boy?

ALBERT: What do you want?
(*The* SPECIAL SECRETARY *releases* ALBERT's *hand and smiles
with satisfaction.* ALBERT *rubs his wrist.*)

SPECIAL SECRETARY: Well, I'm going to ask you a few
questions.

ALBERT: Ask all you want, you won't get any answers.

SPECIAL SECRETARY: Oh, I shall. Come along.
(*The* SPECIAL SECRETARY *takes* ALBERT's *hand and drags
him downstairs like a naughty schoolboy. The others watch this
with amazement, making way for the* SPECIAL SECRETARY
and ALBERT *as they go to the right rear door.*)

BERGMAN: May I ask the meaning of this?

SPECIAL SECRETARY: I'm afraid you'll have to do without this man's assistance for a while. He needs somewhere to think things over . . .

LUISA: Don't put him in the dungeon. Please, I beg. He's – he's ill, can't you see he's feverish!

SPECIAL SECRETARY: He'll soon cool down there . . .

MACOURKOVA: Secretary . . .

SPECIAL SECRETARY: What is it?

MACOURKOVA: Does your room need tidying? Shall I make your bed?

SPECIAL SECRETARY: No.

(*He opens the right rear door and pushes* ALBERT *through it.*)

RENATA: Albert!

(*The* SPECIAL SECRETARY *and* ALBERT, *in the doorway, look at* RENATA *in surprise.*)

Goodbye . . .

ALBERT: Goodbye, Renata.

(*The* SPECIAL SECRETARY *pushes* ALBERT *out firmly and also leaves.* RENATA *runs out by the left rear door, leaving it open.* MACOURKOVA, *also leaving, closes it behind herself. A long pregnant pause.*)

PLEKHANOV: The dance begins . . .

BERGMAN: I warned him.

ULCH: Much as I disagree with him, I feel a certain pity . . .

BERGMAN: It's a lesson he had to learn. Perhaps it'll teach him a little humility.

PLEKHANOV: You needn't have been so hard on him, you know . . .

BERGMAN: I'm only human, Kuzma!

PLEKHANOV: So is he.

(BERGMAN *goes up to* LUISA *and takes her hand.*)

BERGMAN: Luisa – I'm sorry I was indiscreet . . .

LUISA: Don't touch me!

(BERGMAN *moves away from her, embarrassed. A pause.*)

PLEKHANOV: No champagne today, I think . . .

(*Slight pause. Then something takes* LUISA's *attention. She*

191

walks around, sniffing. The others look at her,
uncomprehendingly. Slight pause.)
What's the matter?

LUISA: I smell gas . . .
(*The others begin to walk about sniffing.* LUISA *comes near the
left rear door, sniffs for a while, then suddenly understands.
She runs out through the left rear door, leaving it open. A
moment later her horrified cry is heard.*)
(*Offstage*) Aahhh!
(*They all run towards the left rear door and go out through it,
leaving it open.*)
(*Offstage*) Here, bring her here . . .

PLEKHANOV: (*Offstage*) Wait a minute – not like that – I'll do it
myself . . .

LUISA: (*Offstage*) I should have known rightaway! Poor child!

BERGMAN: (*Offstage*) Well, this is all we needed!

PLEKHANOV: (*Offstage*) She'll come round in a minute . . . here
. . . yes, that's the way . . .

LUISA: (*Offstage*) Brandy! Is there any brandy?
(*The voices grow quiet. A pause. The lights dim, in silence.
Then we hear the fiddle offstage, playing a lyrical melody.*)

ACT V

LUISA *is listening closely as* PLEKHANOV *plays his fiddle. After a while he finishes the piece and puts the fiddle down.*

LUISA: *Do* I know that?

PLEKHANOV: Don't you?

LUISA: It sounds familiar . . .

PLEKHANOV: It should. I once played that to you every night at bedtime. One of those crazy outings of ours at the university.

LUISA: Of course! When we camped out in a hayloft!

PLEKHANOV: Exactly. Only there was no hay in it.

(LUISA *muses for a moment. A pause.*)

LUISA: It's odd. I can remember it so clearly, but I don't feel part of it. As if it happened in a previous lifetime. Have I changed so much? It can't just be age, I'm not that old yet.

PLEKHANOV: To me you're always the same Luisa . . .

LUISA: Nonsense! Don't you remember how marvellously crazy I was? I grabbed at life then, every moment of it, no reservations, no second thoughts, no checking the exits just in case. Whatever caught my interest, I sacrificed everything for it, threw myself into it head first, blew through it like a tornado . . .

PLEKHANOV: Damaging a few items on the way.

LUISA: When did it all come to an end? And why? Look at me now: I've lost the knack of being happy. It's as if I'm in a train and hate the journey and haven't the nerve to jump out. I would have done then. What am I afraid of now?

PLEKHANOV: Remorse?

LUISA: On account of what?

PLEKHANOV: On account, perhaps, of the various items of goods you've damaged in your various jumps?

LUISA: I've never yet met an item of goods, as you put it, which wasn't damaged before I got there.

PLEKHANOV: All damaged goods? I suppose you're right. Only

193

dreams are pure and whole . . . Shall I tell you my attempt
to cope with the problem? What they used to call fortitude.
When I can no longer manage to be happy I try at least not
to be unhappy; and when I can no longer spread more
happiness than others I try at least not to spread more
unhappiness.

LUISA: Do you apply that to your work as well?

PLEKHANOV: Oh yes, there as well. True, we'll spread misery
among the people down there, but then indirectly they're
responsible for spreading misery up here; architecture is
well called the mirror of society. In other words we're
applying the well-known Law of Universal Misery
Exchange.

LUISA: Hardly something to be proud of.

PLEKHANOV: I'd say the only prideworthy item of goods up
here is at present in the dungeon.

LUISA: Pride at second hand.

PLEKHANOV: Better than nothing.

(*A dog begins to bark wildy outside.* PLEKHANOV *and* LUISA
*turn to look towards the right door. The barking stops and there
is a knock on the door.*)

LUISA: Come in!

(*The* FIRST *and* SECOND WOMEN *enter by the right door. The*
SECOND WOMAN *is black. Each carries a string bag containing
three apples. They come down the stairs and stop.*)

FIRST WOMAN: Good afternoon.

LUISA: Good afternoon.

(*Slight pause.*)

FIRST WOMAN: I'd like to see the Project Director, please.

LUISA: I'll see if he's free.

FIRST WOMAN: Thank you.

(LUISA *goes upstairs towards the left door, but before she gets
there* BERGMAN *comes out.*)

BERGMAN: What's going on?

LUISA: You've got visitors.

(BERGMAN *comes down the steps.* LUISA *hesitates, then also
returns.* PLEKHANOV *picks up his fiddle and shuffles off,*

194

glances back curiously at the WOMEN, *then goes out by the right rear door.*)

FIRST WOMAN: Good afternoon.

BERGMAN: Good afternoon.

(*He approaches the* WOMEN *and shakes their hands. Then he indicates that they are to sit down, and sits himself, but the* WOMEN *stay standing.* LUISA *stays to the left in the background. A slight pause.*)

What can I do for you?

FIRST WOMAN: We're the wives of the men who brought the petition . . .

BERGMAN: I remember them.

FIRST WOMAN: We want to ask if we can bring them this fruit.

BERGMAN: But they were released! Weren't they?

(*The* SPECIAL SECRETARY *enters by the left rear door and approaches.*)

SPECIAL SECRETARY: If you please.

(*He takes the bags from the* WOMEN *and tips the apples out on to the table. He shakes out the bags and examines them carefully, puts them aside and with a pen knife from his pocket he begins to cut the apples into pieces. A slight pause, as the others watch him intently.*)

FIRST WOMAN: Excuse me, they're not for you . . .

(*A slight pause as the* SPECIAL SECRETARY *continues.*)

Why are you cutting them up?

SPECIAL SECRETARY: Regulations. There could be a message hidden in one of them.

(*He has now cut up all the apples, which he carefully examines. Then he puts them back into the bags.*)

All clear.

FIRST WOMAN: So will you see that they get them?

SPECIAL SECRETARY: If they don't hinder the investigation they can have them at the proper time.

FIRST WOMAN: When's that?

SPECIAL SECRETARY: Fruit-transmission time.

FIRST WOMAN: When will that be?

SPECIAL SECRETARY: I don't carry all the details on me, you know.

FIRST WOMAN: Well, roughly . . .

SPECIAL SECRETARY: A month, say.

FIRST WOMAN: But they'll be rotten by then!

SPECIAL SECRETARY: I'm not responsible for nature's decaying processes.

(*He takes the bags and begins to climb the stairs. When he is about halfway the* SECOND WOMAN *speaks.*)

SECOND WOMAN: Sir . . .

SPECIAL SECRETARY: What's the matter?

SECOND WOMAN: We wanted to ask something else!

SPECIAL SECRETARY: Yes?

SECOND WOMAN: Why are they back in there after you let them out?

SPECIAL SECRETARY: There's reason to suspect that they are in possession of the facts.

SECOND WOMAN: What facts?

SPECIAL SECRETARY: The real intention of the petition.

SECOND WOMAN: But its real intention was what was written on it.

SPECIAL SECRETARY: So we thought until recently.

SECOND WOMAN: What do you think now?

SPECIAL SECRETARY: Things are surfacing you'd hardly believe.

SECOND WOMAN: What things? We've a right to know.

SPECIAL SECRETARY: You haven't, but I'll tell you anyway. We have evidence to show this was not an innocent petition on behalf of the people, obviously no one would object to that, but a well-timed and carefully engineered signal for the unleashing of mass hysteria, of which you know the tragic consequences. You must see that to avoid such a thing ever happening again we must find the truth and learn from it. Do you have any children?

SECOND WOMAN: Eight.

SPECIAL SECRETARY: There you are then!

(*He quickly crosses the gallery and goes out by the right upper door. A tense pause. Then* LUISA, *after making sure the* SPECIAL SECRETARY *is gone, glances at all the doors then takes out her purse, takes a banknote from it and tries to push it*

into the hands of first the SECOND *then the* FIRST WOMAN.
The WOMEN *want to refuse it.*)

SECOND WOMAN: No, really, no . . .

FIRST WOMAN: It's very nice of you but we can't –

LUISA: Please.

(*There is a confused battle with the note, during which it falls
to the floor.* LUISA *and the* FIRST WOMAN *bend together to
pick it up, bumping their heads. Finally* LUISA *succeeds in
stuffing the note into the* SECOND WOMAN'*s blouse.*)

SECOND WOMAN: Well, thank you –

FIRST WOMAN: Goodbye . . .

(*They exit in embarrassment by the right door.* LUISA *sighs and
wipes her forehead.*)

BERGMAN: Do you know what repercussions that could have?
You must be mad.

LUISA: Don't talk to me! You're despicable . . .

(*She begins to climb the stairs, watched by* BERGMAN.)

BERGMAN: Luisa!

(LUISA *ignores him. A slight pause, then* BERGMAN *runs after
her, catches her and takes her hand.* LUISA *tries to get away.*)

LUISA: Let go! Or I'll start screaming!

BERGMAN: Luisa, you've already behaved stupidly, if you start
a scene you'll only make it worse.

LUISA: Leave me alone, you disgust me.

BERGMAN: What have I done?

LUISA: You ask that after yesterday?

BERGMAN: Oh, that . . .

LUISA: Yes, that. Can you imagine what a shock it must have
been for him? To have you repeating his words in front of
everybody? I knew you were unfeeling, but I never thought
you'd stoop so low. He trusted me, only me. Now his
whole world has collapsed. How do you think he feels
down there?

BERGMAN: All right, it was stupid of me. I got carried away.
It's my nerves, things get on top of me. You've got to
remember what I'd just been through.

LUISA: You?

BERGMAN: The moat! I was within an ace of it!

LUISA: You weren't within an ace of anything.

BERGMAN: So why did you make such a fuss about it?

LUISA: Because I'm an idiot. You put on your melodrama and I fall for it.

BERGMAN: Don't worry, I shan't mention it again; the play is over. I'll do it secretly when you least expect it, maybe at night –

LUISA: If the play were really over you wouldn't be telling me that now.

BERGMAN: They'll find me there one morning. There'll be an argument over who should break the news to you. Plekhanov will do it. You'll cry for a while, reproach yourself for not taking me seriously; remember happier times like the time we sat all night on the pier talking about our lives and drinking muscatel wine – seven years ago was it? – making love as the sun came up and rolling into the sea . . . Or at that international post-modern architecture conference, when we walked through the palm groves night after night long after everyone else had gone . . . Till you have to force yourself to stop thinking about it . . . You'll cry through the funeral, and then – by the way, will you ask Plekhanov to play that song, what's it called? The sad one. Special request . . . Then in time life will return to normal, more or less. Albert will come out of the dungeon and you'll take long nostalgic walks together, talking about me; he'll hardly dare touch you, but his devotion will move you the more. Gradually you'll transfer your feeling from the dead man who no longer needs it to the living one; you'll say to yourself: he always wanted peace, eternal, absolute, definitive peace and now he's got it . . . And if Albert's love endures, which I'm sure it will, he's not superficial, if I seemed to be cynical about his feelings it was only I was so moved . . . even aroused, I'll admit it – to see the excitement in your eyes, your cheeks flushing as you thought of the depths of his emotion, depths a clod like me could never plumb – so if his love endures and his love enters into your soul, becoming the one certainty in your life – then all at once it will happen – you yourselves won't

198

even know how – all at once it will seem so obvious, so simple, so natural and so pure . . . Then that glorious stage of getting to know each other more and more profoundly – that enchantment with each special little feature you discover on each other, a freckle on the underbelly, a cleft ear-lobe, his particular way of shaking all over as he brushes his teeth, the double nail on his foot – and the time will come when you'll forget me completely, I shall evaporate like steam together with all the happy, sad, absurd experiences we went through together, disappear into some kind of black hole somewhere far away in the universe, and that will be my second death, the truly final and truly definitive one . . .

(LUISA, *overcome with emotion, falls to* BERGMAN's *feet, embraces them, puts her head in his lap and begins to sob loudly.* BERGMAN *caresses her tenderly, then he carefully lifts her and kisses her tear-stained eyes. They smile at each other.* BERGMAN *gets up, takes* LUISA *by the hand.*)

Let's go . . .

LUISA: Where?

BERGMAN: You know.

LUISA: Now?

BERGMAN: Why not?

(*He takes* LUISA's *hand and leads here towards the stairs and up. As they are about to go out through the left door a dog begins to bark wildly outside. At this moment the* SPECIAL SECRETARY *bursts in by the right upper door, crosses the gallery and comes down the stairs at a run.* BERGMAN *and* LUISA *look at him in surprise. He sees them.*)

SPECIAL SECRETARY: Call everyone together!

(*He goes quickly to the right door and out, leaving it open.* ULCH *appears at the right upper door,* PLEKHANOV *with his fiddle at the right rear door; both watch what is going on curiously, until the barking subsides.*)

(*Offstage*) Hallo!

SECOND INSPECTOR: (*Offstage*) *Ciao!* Are they ready for me, Mishak?

SPECIAL SECRETARY: (*Offstage*) All ready.

(BERGMAN, LUISA *and* ULCH *come downstairs*, PLEKHANOV
puts his fiddle away. They all look towards the right door.
MACOURKOVA, *panting, runs in by the left rear door. After a
moment the* SECOND INSPECTOR *enters by the right door,
followed by the* SPECIAL SECRETARY, *who closes the door
behind him. They stop on the steps. The* SECOND INSPECTOR
looks at the confused faces with a smile.)

SECOND INSPECTOR: *Ciao!*

BERGMAN: (*Uncertainly*) *Ciao . . .*

SECOND INSPECTOR: Sit down.

(*They all sit down with embarrassment round the table. The*
SECOND INSPECTOR *sits on the steps by the right door, the*
SPECIAL SECRETARY *beside him. The* SECOND INSPECTOR
*takes out a sheet of paper, unfolds it, clears his throat and
begins to read. The* SPECIAL SECRETARY *peers over his
shoulder at the paper.*)

'I'm sure you'll agree that we've come a long way. We have
purged the forward-looking concepts contained within the
previous criticism of early deformation of our strategy of
housing modernization on which the present project is
based, of their later backward-looking disinterpretations,
thus allowing us to purge the strategy itself of its former
deformations. This was not easy; but we can proudly claim
success. Nevertheless we must not rest on our laurels. On
the contrary: the success of our achievements obliges us to
admit openly that the path we have set will achieve its goal
only when we have rolled away the boulder of stagnation
that time has put in its way. . .'

(*He interrupts his reading to extemporize.*)

In other words, time marches on! Not only here, the world
over! And if anyone here thinks otherwise – !

(*The* SPECIAL SECRETARY *gives him an inconspicuous nudge.
He understands, and returns to the paper.*)

'This, of course, needs the co-operation of all concerned. It
has been decided therefore that the development project
must harmonize with the new degree of understanding of
our new-found but temporarily frozen potentialities which
once released must be thrown with all urgency into primal

dialogue as to the optimal alternatives regarding our fu
evolution. This, it goes without saying, demands that we
rid ourselves of fear and conformism, overcome indolence
and indifference, and look truth courageously in the eye,
fearlessly casting outdated ways of thought into the dustbin
and searching freely for new and unconventional
approaches. In this endeavour you have my full support!'
(*He folds up his paper, puts it in his pocket and gets up, as does
the* SPECIAL SECRETARY. *The* SECOND INSPECTOR,
however, feels called on to extemporize again.)
Nothing works without freedom, even my grandmother
knew that, and Mishak's here, yours too, everyone's, black
or white! It's a fact of life, whether you like it or not, so get
your fingers out, otherwise – !
(*The* SPECIAL SECRETARY *leans over to whisper something in
his ear, pointing to his watch. The* SECOND INSPECTOR *nods.*)

MACOURKOVA: Look after yourself, Inspector! We need you!
(*The* SECOND INSPECTOR *goes up to* MACOURKOVA, *puts a
hand on her shoulder and looks into her eyes.*)

SECOND INSPECTOR: Don't worry. *Ciao!*

MACOURKOVA: *Ciao!*
(*The* SECOND INSPECTOR *and the* SPECIAL SECRETARY *go
out by the right door. A slight pause.* LUISA *whispers something
into* MACOURKOVA's *ear,* MACOURKOVA *nods, and they both
go out by the left rear door. The others take their usual places at
the table. A long, oppressive pause.*)

PLEKHANOV: Did you know we have a stork nesting on the
tower?

ULCH: Is that good luck or bad luck?

PLEKHANOV: It depends how you look at it . . .
(*A long, oppressive pause.*)

BERGMAN: While we're on the subject, there's a hole in the
vegetable garden fence. The rabbits are eating the
cabbages.

ULCH: I noticed that. I've been meaning to repair it but things
come up . . .

PLEKHANOV: I'll fix it tomorrow . . .
(*A long oppressive pause.*)

ULCH: The magnolias in the park are in bloom already.

PLEKHANOV: Except for two; a later variety.

(*Pause.* LUISA *and* MACOURKOVA *come in by the left rear door,* LUISA *carrying a tray with five plates of food and cutlery,* MACOURKOVA *a tray with a jug of beer and five glasses. They set everything out on the table, put the trays down and take their seats. Pause. Everyone looks at* BERGMAN, *whose mind is elsewhere. He comes to himself.*)

BERGMAN: *Bon appetit!*

(*They all begin to eat. A long oppressive pause.*)

PLEKHANOV: How's Renata?

LUISA: A bit weak; but she'll probably get up tomorrow.

(*A long oppressive pause.*)

BERGMAN: Is there mint in this?

LUISA: I did put some in. I found some growing in the garden.

BERGMAN: Where in the garden?

LUISA: Right at the back, by the septic tank.

(*A long oppressive pause.*)

ULCH: When I was a lad I used to play the violin. You must lend me yours sometime, Plekhanov.

PLEKHANOV: Of course. Gladly . . .

(*Pause. The* SPECIAL SECRETARY *comes in by the right rear door.*)

SPECIAL SECRETARY: How's the discussion coming along? What conclusions have you reached?

(*An embarrassed pause.*)

BERGMAN: Nothing of substance yet . . .

SPECIAL SECRETARY: Keep at it. Don't be afraid to say what you think!

(*He goes out by the left rear door. A long oppressive pause.*)

PLEKHANOV: I can't wait to get to bed today . . .

BERGMAN: I feel that every day.

(*A long oppressive pause.*)

ULCH: Anyway, it was him she did it for!

PLEKHANOV: Not for you, certainly.

LUISA: She's all right, that's the main thing.

(*A long oppressive pause.*)

BERGMAN: What about tomorrow? Have you worked anything out?

LUISA: I found some mince. So I'll probably make a meat loaf.

ULCH: I'm fond of meat loaf. But only if there's cabbage in it.

LUISA: I don't know if we have any cabbage.

ULCH: No cabbage?

LUISA: The rabbits, you see.

(*Pause. The* SPECIAL SECRETARY *enters by the left upper door and comes down the steps.*)

SPECIAL SECRETARY: Well? Are you full of ideas?

(*Embarrassed pause.*)

BERGMAN: Actually the morning is our time for new ideas . . .

SPECIAL SECRETARY: I wouldn't put it off too long. The situation is grave, the sooner we come up with something new the better.

(*He goes towards the right rear door.*)

LUISA: Secretary . . .

SPECIAL SECRETARY: What's the matter?

LUISA: Don't you think Albert could be let out now?

SPECIAL SECRETARY: I'll ask.

(*He goes out by the right rear door. Pause.*)

BERGMAN: Do you think that was wise?

LUISA: It would have carried more weight if you'd said it.

BERGMAN: I was going to, of course. At the right moment. When I was alone with him or . . .

PLEKHANOV: I think I've worked out where the secret passage went.

ULCH: If there ever was one.

PLEKHANOV: There are several mentions in the archives.

ULCH: For what they're worth.

PLEKHANOV: At a certain spot on the rear wall of that little chamber to the right of the deepest of the cellars, directly beneath the dungeon, there are definite signs of new brickwork . . .

(*A pause. Then the* SPECIAL SECRETARY *and* ALBERT *enter by the right rear door.* ALBERT *looks ill, his face drawn.*)

SPECIAL SECRETARY: So, here he is.

LUISA: Albert!

(The SPECIAL SECRETARY *goes out by the left rear door.*
LUISA *jumps up, rushes over to* ALBERT *and embraces him.*
But ALBERT *shows no reaction.* LUISA *steps back in surprise.*
PLEKHANOV *also gets up, goes to* ALBERT *and gives him a*
friendly slap on the back. ALBERT *shows no reaction.*
PLEKHANOV, *puzzled, goes back to his place in*
embarrassment. Pause.)

BERGMAN: Sit down, everyone, please.

*(*ALBERT *goes to his place mechanically and sits. A pause.)*

ULCH: Bad, was it?

*(*ALBERT *shrugs his shoulders. A pause.)*

LUISA: Why don't you say something? Aren't you glad to be
out?

*(*ALBERT *shrugs his shoulders. A pause.)*

BERGMAN: He's a little confused. Anyone would be.

ULCH: Give him a day or two, he'll be back to normal.

LUISA: Aren't you hungry?

*(*ALBERT *shakes his head. A pause.)*

ULCH: Did you hear about Renata?

*(*ALBERT *shakes his head. A pause.)*

LUISA: She'll be up and about tomorrow. It wasn't your fault.
You're not blaming yourself, are you?

*(*ALBERT *shakes his head. A pause.)*

PLEKHANOV: What about the other two? Have they let them
out?

*(*ALBERT *shakes his head. A pause.)*

LUISA: But they gave them the apples at least?

*(*ALBERT *shakes his head. A pause.)*

BERGMAN: The main thing now is to get a good rest. Get your
thoughts together . . . stabilize your feelings . . . get your
bearings *vis-à-vis* the present situation . . .

(Slight pause. Then ALBERT *rises slowly and as if*
sleepwalking walks towards the stairs. The others watch him as
he mounts the stairs, crosses the gallery and goes out by the right
upper door.)

I didn't expect him to take it so hard . . .

ULCH: It's really done him in.

LUISA: He's sensitive. God knows what they did to him . . .

BERGMAN: Maybe he'll be more careful from now on.
(*Slight pause. Then* PLEKHANOV, *deep in thought, rises and goes towards the stairs.*)

LUISA: Kuzma?
(PLEKHANOV *takes no notice.*)
Are you afraid he might . . .?
(PLEKHANOV, *ignoring her, goes up the stairs, crosses the gallery and out by the right upper door. The* SPECIAL SECRETARY *comes in by the left upper door, comes downstairs to the landing and stops.*)

SPECIAL SECRETARY: I'm looking forward to the morning!
(*They look at him blankly.*)
Your ideas. We need to learn from you, you know.

MACOURKOVA: Won't you join us in our deliberations, Secretary, I'm sure we should benefit!

SPECIAL SECRETARY: I'm afraid I have studies of my own.
(*He goes out by the left door. A very long oppressive pause. Then suddenly crashing sounds are heard outside as of something heavy falling, crashing into obstacles on the way, followed by a very loud dull thud, as if something had hit the ground from a great height. There is total silence for a moment; they look at one another, transfixed.*)

LUISA: Oh, my God!
(*At that moment they all understand what has happened. They run to the rear doors.* BERGMAN *and* LUISA *go out by the left rear door, and* ULCH *and* MACOURKOVA *by the right rear door; both doors are left open. The stage is empty, there is silence. Then* ULCH *and* MACOURKOVA *come in by the left rear door and at the same time* BERGMAN *and* LUISA *by the right rear door. They walk to the middle of the room, frowning, at a solemn, slow pace as if walking behind the coffin at a funeral. They form a half-circle round the table. The* SPECIAL SECRETARY *enters by the left door and stands on the landing.* BERGMAN *slowly crosses to the stairs, climbs them to the landing, steps up to the balustrade and turns to the others as if to give a funeral oration. The* SPECIAL SECRETARY *stands behind him.*)

BERGMAN: Needless to say, we are all deeply affected by what has happened. Not only because of the loss of a much-loved colleague and friend, but because we all carry a share of guilt in regard to his death. We are all responsible for the sad shape our world is in, which has hounded a sensitive man beyond the limits of endurance. We're callous, indolent, indifferent, deaf to the voices of those near and dear to us and blind to their pain. But this bitter consciousness of our complicity has a positive side: we alone, it tells us, can ensure that the death of our friend was not in vain. We alone can give it sense by seeing it as an appeal to us to strive to make a more bearable and more habitable world. Let us therefore promise ourselves at this difficult time that we will never again allow human apathy to rule and destroy. Let us vow never again to connive in the 'redevelopment' of the souls of ourselves or others. Our mission is not to dance to the frivolous beat of an incompetent conductor, but to hold fast to the truth we have found, and dedicate ourselves to the work we have begun. Only thus shall we be true to the moral legacy of this terrible and unexpected death. Only thus can we respond with dignity to the warning voice which calls even now from the depths of the castle moat. Only thus can we show that we hear that voice of reproach and that its message has been understood.

(BERGMAN *comes down the stairs, takes* PLEKHANOV's *fiddle, places it ceremoniously on the table and sits behind it.*)

(*To the fiddle*) We promise you, Kuzma Plekhanov, that we shall not forget!

(*He takes a flower from his breast pocket and places it on the fiddle, assuming a pious pose. The left and right upper doors open simultaneously.* RENATA, *in a nightgown, enters by the left,* ALBERT *by the right upper door. Both stop on the landing. A slight pause.*)

ALBERT: Did you know we have a stork nesting on the tower?
RENATA: I have a sex drive too!

(*A slight pause. Then* LUISA *begins to sob loudly; she goes to the table still sobbing and hysterically grabs the model of the castle with both hands, raises it above her head and with a wild swing down jams it on* BERGMAN's *head so forcefully that his entire face disappears inside.* BERGMAN *continues to stand immobile as if nothing has happened. The others turn to the audience and stare fixedly into the eyes of individual members of it. The song 'Ochi Cherniya' is heard softly, played by a full orchestra. As the stage darkens, the sound grows louder and the house lights begin to brighten. When the stage is dark the music reaches a crescendo, playing at almost deafening volume. Then it suddenly stops; there are several seconds of silence; then music is heard again, but this time, at a reasonable level, Karajan's recording of Strauss's 'Blue Danube' waltz, which will continue until the auditorium is completely empty.)*